WITH A MIGHTY TRIUMPH!

WITH
A
MIGHTY TRIUMPH!

CHRIST'S RESURRECTION AND OURS

RHETT P. DODSON

THE BANNER OF TRUTH TRUST

THE BANNER OF TRUTH TRUST

Head Office
3 Murrayfield Road
Edinburgh, EH12 6EL
UK

North America Office
PO Box 621
Carlisle, PA 17013
USA

banneroftruth.org

© Rhett P. Dodson 2021

*

ISBN
Print: 978 1 80040 004 7
EPUB: 978 1 80040 005 4
Kindle: 978 1 80040 006 1

*

Typeset in 11/14 Adobe Garamond Pro
at The Banner of Truth Trust, Edinburgh

Printed in the USA by
Versa Press Inc.,
East Peoria, IL.

This book is dedicated to

MELTON L. DUNCAN

Christian Gentleman

Presbyterian Elder

Faithful Friend

The resurrection of Christ is the stupendous miracle that validates the truth of the Bible and Christianity. But it is much more than that. It is the actual beginning of the resurrection 'harvest' in which those united to Christ by faith have an assured place—not only in the future at his return in their own bodily resurrection, like his, but also presently as he already shares with them his resurrection life through the presence and work of the Holy Spirit. *With a Mighty Triumph!* explores the rich truths of this resurrection reality in instructive ways that will benefit a wide range of readers.

RICHARD B. GAFFIN, JR
Professor of Biblical and Systematic Theology, Emeritus
Westminster Theological Seminary

CONTENTS

Low in the grave he lay,
Jesus my Saviour,
Waiting the coming day,
Jesus my Lord.

Up from the grave he arose
with a mighty triumph o'er his foes;
he arose a victor from the dark domain,
and he lives forever, with his saints to reign.
He arose! He arose! Hallelujah! Christ arose!

ROBERT LOWRY, 1874

PREFACE

I HAVE always loved Easter. I remember attending Sunrise Service with my father, the family gathered at church, and a Sunday dinner afterwards that was not to be forgotten! I love Easter hymns. My parents raised me to believe the Bible, and so I sang with gusto,

> Low in the grave he lay,
>   Jesus my Saviour,
> Waiting the coming day,
>   Jesus my Lord.
>
> *Up from the grave he arose …*

At times, however, I had my doubts. Did I really believe someone could rise from the dead? Did I really believe Jesus had risen from the dead? As the youngest child of a much older family, I had experienced the loss of several beloved relatives. From my earliest days, death was a dark reality to me. I hadn't just seen it on television shows where I knew it was make believe; I had stood by too many open caskets for someone my age.

'Just believe it,' I told myself. 'It is in the Bible, so it has to be true.' While that was good self-counsel, my struggles with faith in Christ's resurrection existed in a vacuum. For me, Jesus' resurrection was a strange, seemingly impossible event. I had failed to see its purpose. One day, while rummaging through a commentary looking for help, I came across a statement to this effect: When the Saviour hung on the cross and cried out 'It is finished,' three days later God the Father said, 'Amen!' and raised him from the dead. In a moment it all made sense! My theological jargon was limited, but at that instant I understood that the resurrection of Christ was God's vindication of his perfect atoning work on Calvary. The resurrection is the Father's Amen! That stuck with me, and though I cannot now find the original source for that idea, the Lord used it to dispel my doubts and fears.

I now have the privilege of preaching God's glorious Amen! As a minister of the gospel, I celebrate each Lord's Day as Resurrection Sunday. I have hope in the risen Saviour, and God has called me, unworthy though I am, to offer that hope to others. To you, dear reader, I offer that hope in these pages.

With a Mighty Triumph! Christ's Resurrection and Ours is a short series of studies in 1 Corinthians 15, the lengthiest treatment of the resurrection in the New Testament. Paul's treatise is both glorious and challenging. He asserts the reality of Jesus' resurrection in no uncertain terms and defends it with intellectual rigour. But he also refers to baptism for the dead and spiritual bodies. What on earth could these mean? I hope you will read further and find out!

As a pastor-theologian, most of my writing originates in preparation for preaching, and this little book is no exception. I have preached through 1 Corinthians 15 to my patient and loving congregation at Grace Presbyterian Church in Hudson, Ohio. They, like the Thessalonians, receive the Scriptures 'not as the word of men but as what it really is, the word of God' (1 Thess. 2:13). It hardly seems possible that we have searched the pages of the Bible together now for almost a decade. Thank you.

A number of friends have read through these chapters, or parts of them, and offered me helpful feedback and encouragement. They include Stan Gale, Gregg Gorzelle, Joel Huffstutler, and Rick Roth. Gregg deserves a special word of thanks for his extensive and excellent help with editing. Several women have been willing to give me their valuable feedback on these studies as well. Thanks go to my wife, Theresa, my sister, Carolyn McNeely, my administrative assistant, Mary Scherer, and my dear friends Kate Barr and Rachel Bauserman—elect ladies whom I love in the truth (cf. 2 John 1).

Finally, a word about the dedicatee. I could not ask for a better friend than Mel Duncan. I face most problems in life with a two-fold approach: (1.) Pray, and (2.) Call Mel. His friendship, wisdom, counsel, and love are abiding gifts.

As I write this preface, large portions of America are shutting down amid the COVID-19 pandemic. Around the world thousands have died from this virus, and no doubt the death toll will continue to rise. The only hope in the face of death is Jesus, the risen and reigning Jesus. May the Lord use these studies to spread his gospel and glorify his name.

RHETT P. DODSON
Hudson, Ohio
14 March 2020

REMEMBER THE RESURRECTION

1 Corinthians 15:1-11

Now I would remind you, brothers, of the gospel I preached to you, which you received, in which you stand, ² and by which you are being saved, if you hold fast to the word I preached to you—unless you believed in vain.

³ For I delivered to you as of first importance what I also received: that Christ died for our sins in accordance with the Scriptures, ⁴ that he was buried, that he was raised on the third day in accordance with the Scriptures, ⁵ and that he appeared to Cephas, then to the twelve. ⁶ Then he appeared to more than five hundred brothers at one time, most of whom are still alive, though some have fallen asleep. ⁷ Then he appeared to James, then to all the apostles. ⁸ Last of all, as to one untimely born, he appeared also to me. ⁹ For I am the least of the apostles, unworthy to be called an apostle, because I persecuted the church of God. ¹⁰ But by the grace of God I am what I am, and his grace toward me

was not in vain. On the contrary, I worked harder than any of them, though it was not I, but the grace of God that is with me. " Whether then it was I or they, so we preach and so you believed.

IF you had the opportunity to model your local congregation after a church in the New Testament, which one would you choose? I imagine some people would select the church in Rome. They were the recipients of Paul's great letter and were, no doubt, a congregation steeped in the deep doctrines of the faith. Still others may pick the church in Ephesus. They had rich experiences of God's grace. The eyes of their hearts were being enlightened, and they were enjoying the heavenly riches they had in Christ Jesus. I can picture the church at Philippi as a good choice as well. They were, after all, partners with Paul in the gospel, and the apostle seems to have had a closer relationship with that assembly than with any other.

What I don't imagine is anyone saying, 'Oh, I know! Let's be like the church in Corinth!' If you know anything about the churches of the New Testament, then you probably know that Corinth was the most troubled. In fact, you could outline 1 Corinthians with the following headings: Problem Number One, Problem Number Two, Problem Number Three, etc. One after the other, Paul addresses the dilemmas, disagreements, and questions that the Corinthian congregation faced. These include:

• divisions and disputes within the church (1:10–4:21),

- issues of gross immorality (5:1-13; cf. 6:12-20),

- lawsuits against fellow believers (6:1-11),

- questions regarding marriage and purity (7:1-40),

- the delicate spiritual and social situations posed by food offered to idols (8:1–11:1),

- self-centred and disorderly worship (11:2–14:40), and finally,

- some in the church denied the future bodily resurrection of believers (15:1-58).

In each of these instances, the apostle reminds the Corinthians of the gospel again and again. Their problems, their ethical questions, and their doctrinal disputes were a result of failing, in some way, to believe in and live out the truth as it is in Jesus. This is especially evident in dealing with the great theological question regarding the resurrection of the dead. That also stemmed from the same disconnect.

Here is what some people in Corinth were saying: 'Dead people do not, cannot, and will not rise again' (cf. verse 12). Let's be clear about this. These people weren't saying that when a believer dies his or her soul ceases to exist or that he or she doesn't go to heaven to be with God. That issue posed no problem for them at all. It was common in Greek culture to believe in the immortality of the soul. But a dead body brought back to life? That was another issue altogether.

Since this 'no-resurrection' doctrine was starting to gain a foothold in the church, evidently some Christians in Corinth weren't too troubled about this denial of the future resurrection. As long as they could take comfort that departed, believing loved ones were with Jesus and their souls would go to be with Jesus, they wouldn't worry about or argue over what happened to their bodies. They wouldn't concern themselves with theological details and implications. Paul, however, would have none of that. He sees an inseparable connection between the believer's resurrection and that of Jesus Christ himself. To deny the resurrection of believers was to deny the resurrection of Jesus. And to deny the resurrection of Jesus was to deny the very heart of the gospel.

Paul spends the entirety of 1 Corinthians 15 defending the doctrine of the bodily resurrection, but he begins with the resurrection of Jesus and the central role it plays in the gospel. What Paul poses to us in these verses is simply this: If you are a Christian, then at the core of your faith stands the death and resurrection, the bodily resurrection, of Jesus. This is the gospel, and it is the bedrock upon which the doctrine of the resurrection is built. Or, to say it another way, the gospel is Paul's apologetic for the resurrection; and in verses one through eleven he highlighted three of its characteristics.

God's saving message

The first characteristic Paul wants his readers to know is that the gospel is God's saving message. The apostle, like any faithful pastor, is in the reminding business. Those of us who are called to preach and teach the Scriptures don't get to invent new doctrines. That isn't our calling. Our responsibility is to teach and preach the truths the Spirit of God has laid out for us in holy Scripture. We don't, however, just say these things once and go on our way. It is never safe to assume that everyone will remember and apply the truth with earnestness and fidelity. Sin draws our thoughts and affections away from the gospel, and we can easily become twisted in our thinking. This was exactly what had happened to the Corinthians. False teachers had confused them and diverted them from the simplicity and sincerity found in Christ Jesus. And so Paul begins, 'Now I would remind you, brothers, of the gospel' (verse 1a). As Leon Morris has pointed out, these words carry a mild pastoral rebuke.[1] The Corinthians should have remembered the gospel. They should have evaluated every doctrine they heard in light of the gospel, but they had taken their eyes off Jesus and needed their thoughts turned to him once again to focus on Christ and the good news of his person and work.

[1] Leon Morris, *The First Epistle of Paul to the Corinthians.* Tyndale New Testament Commentaries (Grand Rapids: Eerdmans, 1958), 204.

If this gospel is God's saving message, then how are you saved by it? If you were taking an exam that posed that question, how would you answer? Are we saved: (a) by the preaching of the gospel or (b) by the reception of the gospel? The answer has to be 'both' because the gospel, in a sense, has two sides to it.

First, the gospel has a preaching side. The word *gospel* itself means good news, and what is news if it isn't reported? If we wanted to translated verse 1 in a rather wooden manner, we could render it this way: 'Now, I remind you, brothers, of the gospel I "gospelled" to you.' The Bible knows nothing of this good news being hidden away and kept secret. It must be 'gospelled' or proclaimed as good news because God intends it for public consumption. The calling of the apostles and the calling of the church is to herald this message. This point was so important to Paul that he not only begins with this emphasis, he also concludes the first section of the chapter in verse 11 by restating this theme: 'Whether then it was I or they, so we preach and so you believed.'

Second, in addition to the preaching side of the gospel, there is a believing side as well. The only way to personally experience the goodness of the good news is to receive its promises. Paul describes the Corinthians' faith in three ways. 1. They received this message. They accepted it as true and placed their trust in it. They not only acknowledged the truth of Christ that Paul preached, but they also committed their lives to Jesus. The gospel is not information for entertainment or philosophical debate. It is a message that you should receive for its content and power. Reception, however, is more than mental assent. It is a hearty embrace. With your mind, your will, and your affections you cling to Christ because you realize how much you need him.

2. Since they received the gospel, they also stood in it. Paul uses the verb *to stand* two additional times in 1 Corinthians (7:37; 10:12), and in both instances it means to stand firm. The good news of Jesus characterized their present condition as an assembly of believers. The message of Christ not only defined their lives, it stabilized them as well. F. F. Bruce paraphrased this expression as 'the good news ... in the strength of which you stand.'[1] The church in Corinth, like any church, must be established upon the gospel and fixed firm in its truth in order to survive the onslaughts of false teaching.

3. By this gospel the Corinthians were being saved. This expression, at first, sounds rather strange. Aren't Christians already saved? How can they be 'being saved'? When you examine the New Testament, you will discover that it describes our salvation in three tenses—past, present, and future. Grace has a grammar.

---

[1] F. F. Bruce, *The Letters of Paul: An Expanded Paraphrase* (Grand Rapids: Eerdmans, 1965), 113.

When grace speaks in the past tense, it describes those who have placed their faith in Christ as saved from the penalty of sin. That is the reason Paul writes in Romans 8:1, 'There is therefore now no condemnation for those who are in Christ Jesus.' Those who put their faith in Christ alone are justified.

When grace speaks in the future tense, it describes the Christian as one who will be saved from the very presence of sin. The believer's blessed hope is that Jesus will return and take us to be with himself, and so we shall forever be with the Lord (see 1 Thess. 4:13-18). Removed from this fallen world to be in the presence of Jesus, the believer will be glorified like Christ never to sin again.

But grace knows how to speak in the present tense as well. If you are a Christian, then you are being saved from the power of sin. You are being sanctified. The primary evidence of this sanctifying work is a living, ongoing faith in the gospel. In the middle of these declarations, Paul introduces a supposition—'If you hold fast to the word I preached' (verse 2). The little word *if* introduces a reservation or limitation into the text. It in no way casts doubt on the gospel, its truthfulness, or its power. Paul points this *if* at the Corinthians themselves. 'If *you* hold fast to the word,' he wrote, 'then *you* will be saved by it. On the other hand, if *you* do not keep clinging to this message, then *you* have believed in vain.'

Here is the essence of the apostle's argument: I preached the gospel to you. You are being saved by it if you continue to believe the gospel. If, on the other hand, you allow those who deny the resurrection to draw you away from the truth as it is in Jesus then—no matter what you may have professed in the past—you now have an empty, worthless faith. Saving faith in Jesus Christ believes the gospel and keeps on believing the gospel. Faith for the Christian is an ongoing experience. No true Christian can say, 'I used to believe but not anymore.' A Christian says, 'I believed, I am believing, and by the grace of God, I will keep on believing.'

Most of us, sadly, know someone or certainly know of someone who has turned away from the faith. One of the most notorious contemporary examples is the New Testament scholar Bart Ehrman. Early in life, Ehrman was a professing evangelical Christian. He began his formal study of Scripture at Moody Bible Institute and later graduated from Wheaton College. During his graduate studies, however, he began to believe the Bible contained contradictions. As a result, he adopted a liberal approach to Christianity. After following that path for a decade and a half, he gave up all identification as a Christian. Ehrman is now an agnostic who writes books denying the faith he once claimed to believe, a glaring example of someone who believed in vain.

You don't have to be publicly antagonistic to the gospel like Ehrman, however, to turn away from Christ. All you have to do is stop believing. You can continue to attend church and go through the motions. You can continue to lead an upright life, remain faithful to your spouse, and conduct your business with integrity. But if your heart is not firmly fixed on Jesus Christ, then you are in grave danger of falling away forever. The gospel is God's saving message, but you must receive it with a living and abiding faith.

God's primary message

Paul emphasizes a second characteristic in verses 3-8: the gospel is God's primary message. Verse 3 begins, 'For I delivered to you as of first importance what I also received.' Paul uses technical language here to describe the process of being an apostle and handing down the authoritative teaching of the church. He delivers to the Corinthians the message he himself had received. Once again, Paul isn't an inventor or innovator of doctrine. What he received from the Lord Jesus, from the other apostles who had been with Jesus, or what he learned from the pages of Scripture, he passed on to the churches he served.

This apostolic tradition included many things. Think of how vast and deep the Bible is and how much we're taught just in this first letter to the Corinthians. One thing, however, was primary. One element of the apostolic tradition took pride of place. It is of first importance. And that is the gospel itself. This has been Paul's passion all along. That's the reason he wrote in chapter 2, 'I decided to know nothing among you except Jesus Christ and him crucified' (verse 2). In essence Paul says, 'If we're going to keep the main thing the main thing, then the main thing is the biblical and verifiable message of Jesus' death and resurrection.'

The gospel message—this primary message contains four elements, each of which is introduced by the pronoun *that*. First, 'that Christ died for our sins in accordance with the Scriptures' (verse 3). Put yourself in the place of a faithful Israelite who brought his sacrifice to the temple. When he arrived with his unblemished lamb, he placed his hands on its head and confessed his sins. He then took a knife, slit its throat, and watched its body shake and quiver as it bled out and died at his feet. As he looked down at its carcass, lifeless and still, he could say 'That could have been me. My sins deserve death. In fact, that should have been me, but the lamb took my place.'

When Paul writes, 'Christ died for our sins,' he takes our heads in his hands, as it were, and turns our faces to Calvary. There hung Jesus in all of his agony and pain; there hung Jesus bleeding for us. Paul then points to the Son of God and says, 'That should have been you!' Sin brings the penalty of death. And though we are sinners, Jesus died in our place. He died for our sins to take the punishment that we deserved. God's wrath against sin was poured out on Christ rather than on us when he died on the cross.

An historian can tell us that Jesus died. Only God can tell us that Jesus died for our sins. Paul knows this because he listened to the word of God. All of this took place 'according to the Scriptures.' The apostle may well have been thinking about specific passages when he penned these words. Verses like Isaiah 53:5, 6 come to mind.

> But he was pierced for our transgressions; he was crushed for our iniquities; upon him was the chastisement that brought us peace, and with his wounds we are healed. All we like sheep have gone astray; we have turned—every one—to his own way; and the LORD has laid on him the iniquity of us all.

On the other hand, it may have been the entire sweep of redemptive history to which Paul refers.[1] From the fall and the curse right through the Hebrew Scriptures, the hope of Israel was a shepherd who would lay down his life for the sheep, a servant of the Lord who would suffer for the people of God, a lamb who would take away the sins of the world. God's plan was to send a Messiah to Israel through whom all the nations of the earth would be blessed (Gen. 12:1-3).

---

[1] Gordon D. Fee, *The First Epistle to the Corinthians*. The New International Commentary on the New Testament (Grand Rapids: Eerdmans, 1987), 725.

The second 'that' clause informs us that after Jesus died, he was buried (verse 4). Why does Paul think it necessary to include this middle element between the death and resurrection? The burial of Jesus is a key component of the message because it is proof positive that he actually died. He didn't become unconscious, enter a coma, or swoon (as the old liberal theory of the resurrection would have people believe). He actually died. The body of Jesus underwent the physical sufferings of a crucifixion victim, and the soul of Jesus parted from his body. This was real, physical death like any person experiences who passes away.

Christ's burial, however, not only confirmed his death, but it also provided the necessary background to his resurrection. For Paul and the other apostles, the resurrection of Jesus is not wishful thinking. It isn't the product of hallucinations, nor is it a sense that the spirit or ethos of Jesus' teachings would live on among men. The apostolic doctrine of resurrection is that Jesus' dead and buried body came to life again and left the tomb where he had been placed.

This leads to the third 'that' clause: that he was raised (verse 4). The resurrection was, and is, the great vindication of Christ's work. To the naked eye, Jesus merely died like every other crucified criminal. The resurrection, however, serves to attest that his death for our sins was successful! The resurrection is God's seal of approval for the gospel. By the resurrection, Jesus triumphed over death and the powers of sin and hell. He fell under the power of death for a time only to defeat it at last!

One of the greatest theological works to come out of the Puritan era is John Owen's treatise on the atonement. Its title, *The Death of Death in the Death of Christ*,[1] gets to the heart of Easter. Jesus' death meant the death of death. The resurrection is the assurance of that victory and the source of great joy. We celebrate Easter because death has died, and we know death has died because Jesus lives!

Like Christ's death, the resurrection took place 'in accordance with the Scriptures.' If you're familiar with Christian teaching, then it might not seem that unusual to think of Jesus' death as something predicted in the Old Testament. In addition to that, however, Paul says the same about his resurrection. Where would you find this taught? One of the primary places Scripture asserts this truth very clearly is Psalm 16:10. In that psalm David wrote, 'For you will not abandon my soul to Sheol, or let your holy one see corruption.'

You may say, 'Yes, but that's David writing about himself. He had hope that he would see God.' Certainly David had that hope, but this can hardly be David writing about himself because he says, 'you will not … let your holy one see corruption.' David

---

[1] John Owen, *The Death of Death in the Death of Christ* (1684; Edinburgh: Banner of Truth Trust, reprint 1959).

did see corruption. The people of Jesus' day could visit his grave. David was not speaking for himself in this psalm. As a prophet, he was speaking the words of the Christ who was to come! Peter made this clear when he preached on the day of Pentecost.

> 'Brothers, I may say to you with confidence about the patriarch David that he both died and was buried, and his tomb is with us to this day. Being therefore a prophet, and knowing that God had sworn with an oath to him that he would set one of his descendants on his throne, he foresaw and spoke about the resurrection of the Christ, that he was not abandoned to Hades, nor did his flesh see corruption. This Jesus God raised up, and of that we all are witnesses' (Acts 2:29-32).

Peter's reference to witnesses leads us to the fourth 'that' clause in Paul's message to the Corinthians, the fourth facet of the good news. We typically define the gospel in terms of Jesus' death, burial, and resurrection, but Paul reminds us not to leave out the Saviour's post-resurrection appearances. They serve to verify that he rose from the tomb. Paul begins with Peter and the Twelve (verse 5a). Called here by his alternate name Cephas, Peter saw the risen Jesus as did the rest of the disciples. The Gospels record several of Jesus' appearances to the disciples (Luke 24:36-53; John 20:19-23), and the two men on the road to Emmaus had already heard that Jesus had appeared to Peter (Luke 24:34).

In addition, Paul lists four more appearances of the Lord Jesus to emphasize that this biblical message was verifiable. These additional appearances include the following: an appearance to more than five hundred at one time, to James, to all the apostles, and to Paul himself. We're not sure when the appearance to the five hundred plus brothers occurred. It may have been in Galilee (cf. Matt. 28:16-18) or this may be the only reference to it in the New Testament. What is significant about the testimony of this large group is that most of them were still alive when Paul wrote this letter. Why was it important for Paul to stress this point? Because it meant you could go and ask these people what they saw. The account of the resurrection was not hearsay that had been handed down for generations.

Next, Paul lists James. There are five, possibly six, men in the New Testament with the name of James. Many scholars believe this is a reference to Jesus' brother. He had not been a follower of Christ before the resurrection, but afterwards he not only became a believer but a leader of the church in Jerusalem. Leon Morris believes 'that it was this appearance which led to his conversion and through him to that of his brothers.'[1]

The reference to 'all of the apostles' includes more than the original twelve. Others who knew the Lord Jesus and were witnesses of his resurrection were also

[1] Morris, *First Corinthians*, 207.

called to be apostles (cf. Acts 1:21-22; 4:33; 1 Cor. 9:1). This group included Matthias, Judas' replacement (Acts 1:26); Barnabas (Acts 14:14); James, the Lord's brother (Gal. 1:19); Epaphroditus (Phil. 2:25); and a group called 'our brothers' (2 Cor. 8:23).[1]

Last of all, Christ appeared to Paul. This statement refers to the account of his conversion on the road to Damascus (Acts 9:1-9). He describes this appearance 'as to one untimely born.'[2] Paul portrays himself this way because he did not live and travel with the other apostles who knew Jesus during his earthly ministry. It appears Paul's conversion did not take place until several years after Christ's ascension. Thus he was not 'born' when the others were. Jesus started his apostolic band many years earlier, but when Paul met him on the Damascus road he became as much of an apostle as any of the rest. It was an untimely birth but a live birth nonetheless!

Let's step back for a moment and remind ourselves why verses 3-8 are so important. The gospel that Paul preached and the Corinthians professed to believe was

---

[1] For Christ's appearance to all of the apostles, see John 20:26ff. and Acts 1:1ff.

[2] The term translated *untimely* can refer to a miscarriage or premature birth, and in some cases even to an abortion. Some conjecture that this description was one used about Paul by his opponents which he, in turn, borrows as a sign of humility. He was 'this "abortion" of an apostle, as some call me.' Bruce, *Letters of Paul*, 113. I find the explanation above more satisfactory.

a gospel about Jesus' death, burial, and bodily resurrection. Paul interpreted those great redemptive events for us. Jesus died for our sins and rose again according to the Scriptures. This biblical and theological message was not mere wishful thinking. It was historically verifiable. More than five hundred people could attest to it.

The number is significant because in a Jewish court of law two or three eyewitnesses could establish the certainty of a verdict. Two or three witnesses could even secure the death penalty (see Deut. 17:6; 19:15; cf. 2 Cor. 13:1). In a modern-day courtroom, if three eyewitnesses testified they had seen you commit a crime, then it would be difficult, if not downright impossible, to prove your innocence. Imagine you were on trial and over five hundred eyewitnesses made that claim. The judge would say, 'You can't refute the weight of this first-hand evidence.'

The implications of what Paul writes in these verses for the veracity of the resurrection cannot be underestimated. The bodily resurrection of Jesus that first Easter morning is one of the most well-supported facts of history. Now, let the weight of that evidence bear down on your own soul. The resurrection of Jesus is either the most elaborate hoax anyone has ever pulled off, or it is the best news you could ever hear.

God's gracious message

Paul highlights the third and final characteristic of the gospel in verses 9-11. The gospel is God's gracious message. The personal reference in verse 8 prompts Paul to think about his own conversion and subsequent ministry, which he proceeds to describe in verses 9 and 10. How did he summarize his life and work? He condenses it all to one word: *grace*. If you look closely at these verses, you will see that he refers to God's grace three times and captures for us the powerful effect grace has on our lives.

First, grace lowers the estimation we have of ourselves. In true humility, Paul sees himself as the least of the apostles. Not only is he 'untimely born' (verse 8), he feels unworthy to be numbered among their band. He is almost ashamed to be mentioned along with such a godly group of men because he had persecuted the church. Paul did not live under the defeat of his past sins, but he did remember them. He remembered the way he had hounded and abused Christians. By remembering what he had been, he kept himself humble before God and before others.

When we puff ourselves up with pride, we have forgotten the gospel of grace. We have failed to remember our sin and the great debt we owe to God's sheer mercy. Show me a proud man, and I will show you a man who knows little to nothing about the grace of God. You and I build ourselves up in our own eyes when we forget the pit of sin and despair from which Jesus rescued us.

George Whitefield was perhaps the most celebrated preacher of the eighteenth century. His eloquent preaching so impressed Benjamin Franklin that he gladly listened to Whitefield even though he didn't believe the message. It was said that Whitefield could move people to deep emotion simply by the way he said *Mesopotamia*. We might even call him the first 'celebrity preacher.' But Whitefield was a man of great grace, a man with a deep experience of his own sin and the power of God's goodness. We see the evidence of this when he wrote, 'Let the name of Whitefield perish, but Christ be glorified. Let my name die everywhere, let even my friends forget me, if by that means the cause of the blessed Jesus may be promoted.'[1] Grace humbles us by reminding us that we are less than the least (cf. Rom. 12:3).

Second, grace not only humbles us in our own estimation, it also exalts the transforming power of God. Paul saw himself as nothing, but he was a believer, an apostle, a preacher of the gospel. And he was all of those things by the grace of God. Everything Paul was, everything he accomplished, every gift he possessed he attributed to the sheer goodness of God's mercy.

[1] Arnold Dallimore, *George Whitefield: God's Anointed Servant in the Great Revival of the Eighteenth Century* (Wheaton: Crossway, 1990), 154.

Without the unmerited favour of God shown to him in the resurrected Jesus, he would have been nothing.

This is the testimony of every child of God. The believer who has any experience of his sin and of God's salvation is compelled to say, 'I'm nothing in my own eyes. And it's okay if I'm nothing in your eyes. But whatever I am, whatever good you may see in my life, whatever word of kindness might come from my lips or act of love from my hands, you can chalk it all up to God's unmerited favour. I don't think I'm anything, but if I am anything it is surely by grace alone.' Grace humbles us and exalts the Lord Jesus, and that is exactly what it is supposed to do.

The third thing Paul says about this grace is that it energizes the service we render to Christ. The apostle was concerned that if the Corinthians abandoned the bodily resurrection that his evangelistic efforts among them would have been in vain (verse 2). But he could assure them that God's grace toward him was not in vain. Paul was working out his own salvation with fear and trembling (cf. Phil. 2:12). His faith was active. He was 'being saved' (cf. verse 2). Not only was God's grace to him 'not in vain' but, on the contrary, he worked harder than any of the other apostles (verse 10). But even the strenuous effort he put in day after day was fuelled by God's grace. Paul isn't patting himself on the back. 'I worked,' he writes, but it wasn't I 'but the grace of God that is with me' (cf. Col. 1:29).

Christian service happens this way. We give to God what he first gives to us. It is like a child going to her father and asking, 'Daddy, may I please have $10?' 'Why does a little girl like you want all that money?' the father replies. 'Oh, Daddy, I want to buy you a birthday present!' What does the father do? He reaches into his pocket and pulls out the money.[1] The little girl loves her daddy. She wants to give him a nice present for his birthday, but she has no resources of her own. That's what we're like. We want to serve our heavenly Father, but how on earth can we do it? We serve only by grace, and our heavenly Father delights to give that grace to us.

Grace humbles us, exalts God, and energizes our service. Finally, in verse 11, grace keeps us focused on the goal. Most commentators will tell you that when Paul reached verse 11, he reverted back to verse 8 and to pick up the thread of his argument from there. Thus verses 9 and 10 constitute a personal interlude, a reflection on his own experience. I'm not altogether sure that is exactly what Paul has in mind. Verse 11 is actually the inference drawn from this personal interlude. It isn't divorced from verse 8 where Paul lists himself with the other eyewitnesses. His purpose, however, is to keep all of his readers focused on the goal. Yes, he

---

[1] Archibald Robertson and Alfred Plummer, *A Critical and Exegetical Commentary on the First Epistle of St Paul to the Corinthians*, Second edition. The International Critical Commentary (Edinburgh: T&T Clark, 1982), 342.

worked harder than all of the apostles, but that wasn't the point. The person preaching the gospel isn't what matters most. The issue is the gospel itself, and the goal of the gospel is that it be preached and believed.

Paul brings the first part of his defence of the resurrection to a conclusion with the words of verse 11. His point is not that he was better than the other apostles. Far from it. Whether he was the one preaching the gospel, or it was one of the others to whom Jesus appeared, the message never changes. The message is,

Jesus Christ has been raised from the dead!

That gospel message is the foundation of all our hopes for forgiveness, for salvation, for freedom from guilt and shame. And that same message is the foundation of our hope that one day we too shall rise.

2

IMAGINE THERE'S NO EASTER

1 CORINTHIANS 15:12-19

Now if Christ is proclaimed as raised from the dead, how can some of you say that there is no resurrection of the dead? [13] But if there is no resurrection of the dead, then not even Christ has been raised. [14] And if Christ has not been raised, then our preaching is in vain and your faith is in vain. [15] We are even found to be misrepresenting God, because we testified about God that he raised Christ, whom he did not raise if it is true that the dead are not raised. [16] For if the dead are not raised, not even Christ has been raised. [17] And if Christ has not been raised, your faith is futile and you are still in your sins. [18] Then those also who have fallen asleep in Christ have perished. [19] If in Christ we have hope in this life only, we are of all people most to be pitied.

JOHN LENNON sang,

> Imagine there's no heaven
> It's easy if you try
> No hell below us
> Above us only sky
> Imagine all the people living for today.

Imagine.

C. S. Lewis described the land of Narnia as a place where it was always winter but never Christmas.

Imagine.

Lennon wanted his generation to strive for peace and harmony without the burden of God. Lewis, on the other hand, saw the cold, dead bleakness of a world without God. Imagine with me a combination of both. Imagine a world of perpetual winter. Above this world hangs a cold, steel-grey sky. Because it is always winter, there will be no spring. Because there is no Christmas, there will be no Easter. Imagine there's no Easter. That, in essence, is what Paul invites us to do in this passage.

It seems that people within the church at Corinth believed in the immortality of the soul. That was a common doctrine accepted throughout the Greek world. Some, however, denied that the bodies of the dead would ever be raised (verse 12). In verses 1-11 Paul defends the resurrection as essential to the gospel and in complete keeping with what Scripture teaches. He also appeals to the eyewitness evidence. Many people saw the resurrected Christ; in fact, more than five hundred people saw him at one time (verse 6). The evidence for the resurrection was irrefutable.

Next, Paul moves from a positive proclamation of the resurrection to present the consequences if there were no resurrection. His basic argument is this: If we preach Jesus' resurrection as an essential element of the gospel, and if we can prove the resurrection from the Bible and eyewitness testimony, then how can you say, 'There is no resurrection from the dead'? (verse 12).

Paul wants the logic of the resurrection to sink into the Corinthians' minds and to weigh on their consciences. The Christian faith as a whole and your salvation as an individual rest on the bodily resurrection of Jesus. If the dead do not rise, then Christ has not been raised (verse 13). If Christ has not been raised, then the consequences are disastrous. Paul lists those consequences in verses 12-19, and I want us to give each of them a one-word title.

Empty

The title for the first consequence is *empty*. If you've ever had to buy a gift for a special occasion and, after hours of shopping, either couldn't find what you were looking for or couldn't afford what you found, then you know how disappointing it can be to return home empty-handed. To impress on the believers in Corinth the seriousness of the 'no-resurrection' doctrine, Paul reminds his readers that if Christ has not been raised from the dead, then the church is left disappointingly empty-handed in two of its primary spheres: preaching and faith.

Without the doctrine of the resurrection, gospel preaching is void of any saving content. 'Our preaching,' wrote Paul, 'is in vain.' The word the apostle chose for preaching is a fairly rare term in the New Testament. It occurs only nine times.[1] Its meaning can focus on either the act of preaching or the content of what one preaches. Paul proclaimed Christ crucified, and he preached this message as one sent by God with a divine commission.[2] The verb related to this noun occurs in verse 12 where Paul writes, 'Christ is proclaimed as raised.' The content of the message drives the medium of preaching. The call to present Christ is the call to announce the good news, to make a public proclamation, but this public declaration must have specific content. Preaching must have something worthwhile to say; otherwise, the church becomes an echo chamber. The outward form of preaching must have the internal content of Jesus Christ crucified, buried, and raised from the dead (cf. verses 3, 4).

[1] Matt. 12:41; Mark 16:8; Luke 11:32; Rom. 16:25; 1 Cor. 1:21; 2:4; 15:14; 2 Tim. 4:17; Titus 1:3. The occurrence in Mark 16:8 is in a textual variant.

[2] Verlyn D. Verbrugge, ed. *The NIV Theological Dictionary of New Testament Words* (Grand Rapids: Zondervan, 2000), 684.

Without the reality of God's redeeming love in Christ demonstrated in the resurrection, evangelical declarations aren't good news at all. Without the resurrection, they are merely sounds that fade in the air.

If empty preaching is proclamation without substance, mere words with no meaning, then the clear implication of Paul's statement is, 'Without the resurrection, there is no need to preach because there is nothing to preach.' If there is no Easter, then there is no reason to gather as an assembly of believers on the first day of the week. If there is no Easter, then church and worship and preaching are all just a waste of time. Without the resurrection of Christ, we have no gospel to proclaim. If you rob the church of the resurrection, then you rob it of its primary task in the world—missions (cf. Matt. 28:19, 20)! Apart from the bodily resurrection of Jesus, the church has nothing to offer the world but moralistic maxims with no more authority than any other religious or philosophical system.

Paul goes further. If his preaching was vain, then so too was their faith (verse 14b). What good is faith in a risen Saviour if there is no risen Saviour? If your creed tells you that Jesus has been raised from the dead but that has not happened and his body still lies in a tomb in Israel, then your faith is empty-handed. To have empty faith is to engage in make-believe. If there is no Easter, then Christianity is no better than a fairy tale. For faith to be anything more than wishful thinking, it must have an objective, historical basis in what God has done in Christ for our salvation.

In the past, it has been common for some theologians and pastors to talk about an 'Easter Faith.' By that expression they meant a faith that believes in the spiritual message of Easter but not in the historical, time-and-space fact of Jesus' bodily resurrection. That kind of 'Easter Faith,' however, is nothing more than positive thinking. It may make a person feel better about himself for a while. It may bolster a temporary optimistic outlook, a cheery disposition, an effort to pretend that everything isn't as bad as it may seem. At the end of the day, however, positive thinking runs headlong into the wall of hard reality. Without the true and lasting hope the gospel offers, no true and lasting hope exists.

Paul links the emptiness of preaching to the emptiness of faith because preaching and faith stand or fall together. Faith comes by hearing and hearing by the preaching of Jesus (Rom. 10:17). No one can call upon the Lord to be saved unless he or she believes the Lord is able to save. In addition, no one will believe in God's saving power unless that person hears the testimony of the gospel. Finally, no one can hear the gospel unless someone is sent to proclaim it (Rom. 10:13-15). The apostle had already reminded his readers, 'Whether then it was I or they, so we preach and so you believed' (1 Cor. 15:11).

Preaching and faith are, in some ways, like two sides of the same coin. That is true whether the faith to which Paul refers is the faith—the content of the Christian message—or one's personal trust in the veracity of that message. Neither preaching and the faith nor preaching and one's own commitment to Christ can be torn the one from the other. If the church is to give a robust and powerful witness to the truth as it is in Christ, then a recovery of the faith will lead to a revival of preaching; and that, in turn, will lead to personal transformation. That, in a nutshell, is the story of the Protestant Reformation. As Luther, Calvin, Knox, and a host of others recovered the biblical doctrines of the faith, God raised up men to proclaim the truth. Biblical preaching led to the spiritual change that took place in the sixteenth and seventeenth centuries.

Biblical preaching, however, has to fight for survival in every generation. We often hear that authoritative declarations or any kind of earnest preaching is outdated. It is too old fashioned to be accepted by the world. Many folks seem content with a little talk, a few practical tips, and some positive affirmations to make them feel better about their lives. But will that kind of preaching bear witness to the risen Lord? Will it build mature, godly Christians? As the church in the West continues to decline, we need to recapture the apostolic joy and power of believing in and heralding forth the risen Christ. We need to go back to our essential

gospel roots and realize not only the devastating consequences of denying them but the unsurpassed delight
that comes from proclaiming them.

When the Scottish pastor Alexander Whyte asked
why earlier generations had produced such godly and
mature Christian men and women, he listed persecution, Reformation theology and masculine, Pauline
preaching![1] It is this third area that especially seems
lacking today. In the West, we are starting to feel more
and more pressure as Christians. The persecution isn't
as severe as others have faced, but open opposition to
the faith is on the rise. Books on Reformed theology
abound. We have access to solid doctrine. The church
suffers, however, from a lack of manly, Pauline, exposi-
tory, theological, demanding, hard-thinking, and
hard-hitting preaching.

If we are going to give witness to the reality and
glory of Christ's resurrection, then we must pray for
and work for the recovery of this kind of preaching!
Pastors bear a huge weight of responsibility for this
recovery, the responsibility of prayer and the hard
work of biblical exegesis that goes into sermon preparation. Individual Christians and congregations play
a vital role in this recovery as well. They have a duty
to pray for their pastors. Do you pray for your pastor

[1] David Hay Fleming, 'Dr Whyte and Samuel Rutherford,' *Criti-
cal Reviews Relating Chiefly to Scotland*, 1912, 350, quoted in Iain
H. Murray, *The Puritan Hope: Revival and the Interpretation of
Prophecy* (Edinburgh: Banner of Truth Trust, 1971), 86.

during the week as he sits at his desk and digs into the Scriptures? Do you ask God to fill him and anoint him and use him? Your responsibility doesn't stop there. It begins with prayer, but it includes your presence as well. A recovery of preaching requires Christians to be in the pews on a regular basis, to discipline themselves to be under the preached word. Robust, biblical preaching won't necessarily be popular. If the current church scene teaches us anything, then it teaches us that shallow, man-centred, feel-good messages are the way to 'build' the church. That kind of message may fill buildings, but it will leave people with empty hearts. It may draw crowds, but it isn't equipped to declare from the rooftops the glories of a risen, ascended, and reigning Lord!

False

Next Paul presents the opposite side of empty preaching, a consequence we can label *false*. 'We are even found to be misrepresenting God' (verse 15). Without the reality of the resurrection, the apostles and all of the other five hundred plus eyewitnesses were false witnesses in the end. The term the ESV renders *misrepresenting* is more literally *bearing false witness* (cf. KJV, NIV, NET, CSB). This particular word occurs only here and in Matthew 26:60 where it describes the false witnesses who came forward to testify against Jesus. To bear false witness is to tell something that isn't true. It is to misrepresent the truth or, in this case, to misrepresent God himself.

Paul grounds this statement, however, in the second half of the verse, 'Because we testified about God that he raised Christ, whom he did not raise if it is true that the dead are not raised' (verse 15). How should we understand the phrase about God? Did Paul mean that those who proclaimed Jesus as risen were bearing false witness because they testified against God? That would be a fairly common translation of the preposition the apostle used. Could, however, Paul mean that God had sent the apostles to testify; and if Christ hasn't been raised then God himself sent them on an errand of falsehood?[1] If the first were true, then the apostles would bear the blame for misleading their hearers. If the second were true, then God would bear the blame!

In either case, the consequences are disastrous because they are blasphemous. Whether one tells a lie about or against God, or whether one asserts that God sent him to bear a false testimony, he defames the glorious name of the Almighty. Paul wants the Corinthians to know that a denial of the resurrection of Christ left them in an untenable position. If the dead will not be raised, then Jesus has not been raised. If Jesus has not been raised, then the gospel isn't good

---

[1] John Calvin, *Commentary on the Epistles of Paul the Apostle to the Corinthians*. Translated by John Pringle (Grand Rapids: Baker, reprint 2003), vol. 2, 19-20.

news but a farce, and the apostles are charlatans, hawkers of a cheap and meaningless Messiah. The gospel is an empty enterprise without the reality of history as its foundation. 'For if the dead are not raised, not even Christ has been raised' (verse 16).

In light of Paul's argument, we see the church's calling to bear a true witness to God and gospel. Had the Corinthians maintained a firm grip on the trustworthiness of Scripture and the infallibility of the apostolic witness to the gospel, they would not have strayed into questioning or denying the doctrine of the bodily resurrection. Fidelity to Christ requires us to believe in and proclaim the inerrancy of the Bible.

I became fascinated by the doctrine of Scripture when I was a teenager and bought two books that played a significant role in the development of my thinking. The first was Benjamin B. Warfield's *The Inspiration and Authority of the Bible*. The second was Harold Lindsell's *The Battle for the Bible*. While Warfield laid a solid foundation for belief that the Bible is God's trustworthy word, Lindsell chronicled the struggle for this doctrine that occurred in evangelicalism in the 1960s and '70s. When I read Lindsell, I was convinced that the battle for the Bible had been fought and won. Christians believed the Scriptures were from God and, therefore, without any error. The battle for the Bible, however, is never over. In each generation doubts as to its veracity are raised both from within the church and from without. We must reclaim faith in the truthfulness of the Bible in each generation.

The inerrancy of Scripture assures us that the facts we read in the Bible are true. That, of course, is essential. If the Bible isn't true in what it asserts, then we should give up on Christianity altogether. Belief in inerrancy, however, must take us further. The Bible not only gives us the facts; it interprets those facts for us. It tells us what happened in redemptive history: Jesus died and rose again. It also tells us why these events occurred: Christ died for our sins (verse 3), and he was raised again for our justification (Rom. 4:25). Furthermore, through its interpretations, the Scriptures reveal the character of God. They give us a true picture of what he is like. We need to embrace the doctrine of the Bible's inerrancy not only because we need to know what actually happened, we also need inerrancy so we know whom to trust!

The inerrancy of Scripture isn't a mere theoretical notion; it is a most pointed and practical truth for the believer's walk with God. As we rely upon the Lord in our daily lives, the effects of that faith become evident in the way we handle the tragedies, heartaches, and trials that come to us. Christ gives hope in the face of disaster and discouragement and as we live out that hope, our testimonies serve as a true witness that God has raised him from the dead.

Futile

We may summarize the third consequence of denying the resurrection with the word *futile*. If Jesus' body still lies in a tomb in Israel, then you have a futile faith and stand under a guilty verdict. In verse 14, Paul describes faith apart from the resurrection of Christ as vain or empty. It has no content. In verse 17, the apostle asserts that if Christ Jesus has not been raised from the dead, then faith is also fruitless. Such a 'faith' is not only void of real substance, it is useless. It doesn't accomplish what God intends faith to do. What does God intend faith to do? We could answer that question in many ways from many verses in the Bible, but in this context Paul's focus is on faith's role in salvation and forgiveness.

God has chosen faith to be the means by which we receive his free gift of pardon and everlasting life. Scripture bears witness to this truth over and over again. For example, to the Philippian jailer Paul and Silas said, 'Believe in the Lord Jesus, and you will be saved, you and your household' (Acts 16:31). Paul also wrote to the church in Ephesus, 'For by grace you have been saved through faith. And this is not your own doing; it is the gift of God' (Eph. 2:8). To the church in Rome he asserted, 'Therefore, since we have been justified by faith, we have peace with God through our Lord Jesus Christ' (Rom. 5:1).

Faith doesn't earn anything from God. Believing isn't a good work that he rewards. Faith is the empty hand that receives, the eyes that look, the mouth that calls upon the name of the Lord. By faith we trust. We believe what Scripture tells us about Christ's saving work on our behalf, and we commit our souls into his gracious and saving hands.[1] If Christ has not been raised from the dead, then committing the safekeeping of your soul to him is a pointless act. It means nothing and will accomplish nothing.

That is the reason Paul concludes verse 17 with the words, 'and you are still in your sins.' If the dead do not rise, and Christ's body still lies in a tomb, then you remain under a record of guilt. In fact, without Christ's resurrection as the vindication of his atoning death, sin has no solution. The burdened conscience has no relief. A 'Jesus' that remains dead has no power to forgive.

Willi Marxsen was a German pastor who became a well-known New Testament scholar. He wrote a book on the resurrection of Jesus,[2] but in it he taught that the resurrection is a spiritual event rather than a bodily, physical event that took place in history. For Marxsen, the resurrection is a subjective experience that takes place in a believer's heart. Marxsen, however, missed

---

[1] John Murray defined saving faith as 'a whole-souled movement of self-commitment to Christ for salvation from sin and its consequences.' *Redemption: Accomplished and Applied* (Edinburgh: Banner of Truth Trust, 2016), 108.

[2] Willi Marxsen, *The Resurrection of Jesus of Nazareth* (Philadelphia: Fortress, 1970).

Paul's point. Without a physical resurrection of Jesus, there can be no spiritual resurrection or conversion or new life in the heart of anyone. If Christ has not been raised, then we are still lost and undone. We are still in our sins and without hope.[1]

If the premise of verse 17 were true and Jesus Christ remained dead, then this would be the darkest, most damning passage in all the Bible because we are all conscious, to one degree or another, of our sin and guilt. We need, therefore, to be well acquainted with the gospel and the liberating hope it offers. Because Christ has been raised again for our justification (Rom. 4:25), you and I can be declared righteous in the sight of God. We can have the record of our sins purged and be right with God. The Westminster Shorter Catechism summarizes this truth so well when, in answering question 33, 'What is justification?' it states, 'Justification is an act of God's free grace, wherein he pardoneth all our sins, and accepteth us as righteous in his sight, only for the righteousness of Christ imputed to us, and received by faith alone.'

When we live in the freedom from guilt Christ offers us, then we say to the world, 'Jesus lives!' We are not, therefore, afraid to face our sin. In fact, we ask God to show us the ways we have displeased him

---

[1] Simon J. Kistemaker, *Exposition of the First Epistle to the Corinthians.* New Testament Commentary (Grand Rapids: Baker, 1993), 541-42.

so that we can confess our transgressions and enjoy his free pardon. We live with assurance, knowing that if we are forgiven by God, if we are justified and declared righteous in his sight, then we are certain of everlasting life.

Lost

The term *lost* captures the fourth consequence of denying the resurrection. In verse 18, Paul turns the focus away from the Corinthians and their current condition to the members of the church who have passed away. If Christ has not been raised, 'Then those also who have fallen asleep in Christ have perished.'

'Those who have fallen asleep' is a metaphorical description of believers who have died. They have fallen asleep in Jesus. This language occurs several times in the New Testament, beginning with Jesus using the phrase himself. Christ refers to Lazarus' death as his having fallen asleep (John 11:11). When Christ was raised, many tombs were opened, and the bodies of saints who had fallen asleep were raised (Matt. 27:52). When Stephen was stoned to death, he fell asleep (Acts 7:60). Here in this very chapter Paul appeals to the massive eyewitness accounts of Christ's resurrection and notes that most of those people were still alive at the time he wrote this letter, though some have fallen asleep (1 Cor. 15:6). Paul also makes extensive use of this metaphor for death in

1 Thessalonians 4:13-15. This expression in no way implies that Paul or any other apostle believed in soul sleep or the unconscious existence of the individual between death and the resurrection. Paul could not be clearer on this issue than his statement in 2 Corinthians 5:8. When the believer's soul is away from the body, it is at home with the Lord. When the term *sleep* occurs in the New Testament in relation to death, it is always an image to describe the state of the body as it awaits the day of resurrection.

What did Paul mean, however, when he wrote these believers 'have perished'? Did he propose they had simply ceased to exist? That meaning would not fit the cultural context since the Greeks had no difficulty believing in the immortality of the soul. Perhaps he meant the disintegration of the body. Believers who die never rise again. Their bodies return to dust, and that is the end. That meaning would fit the general context and be in line with the 'no-resurrection' doctrine some were peddling. The verb Paul uses could mean either of those options, but it also occurs in the New Testament to describe the perishing of the lost in hell. See, for example, the contrast between 'perishing' and 'everlasting life' in John 3:16 (cf. 1 Cor. 1:18). This meaning most naturally follows from verse 17. If believers die without the hope of Christ's victory over sin and death, then they die in their sins and perish like the rest of mankind, lost and undone.

Like the other consequences Paul lists in this passage, the death of believers gives us the opportunity to maintain a powerful witness to the reality of Jesus' resurrection if we demonstrate to the world how to grieve with hope. The simultaneous existence of both sadness and hopefulness in the human heart is a mystery to those who do not know Christ. They can't understand how Christians can weep and yet have the assurance that all is not lost. We react in both of those ways because we know the deep anguish that death brings, but we also have the confidence that Christ's life gives to us. This was the very point Paul made in his first letter to the church in Thessalonica. He wrote,

> But we do not want you to be uninformed, brothers, about those who are asleep, that you may not grieve as others do who have no hope. For since we believe that Jesus died and rose again, even so, through Jesus, God will bring with him those who have fallen asleep (1 Thess. 4:13, 14).

I originally wrote this chapter the week after Easter. On Easter Monday, I received a message that a friend of many years had suffered a stroke. The next day word came that he had undergone emergency surgery. The following day the doctors said he would not regain consciousness. On Thursday, he was removed from life support systems and passed away. As my wife communicated with his wife in the midst of all the stress and sorrow, when his wife knew that they would take him off life support the next day, she said, 'Tomorrow I have to let him go to Jesus.' That is what it means to face death with hope, with the assurance that those who sleep in Christ are not lost. Every time we respond with that confidence we proclaim, 'Jesus lives!'

Pitiable

The best term I know to summarize the fifth and final consequence of denying Christ's resurrection is the word *pitiable*. With a final *if*, Paul introduces his last conditional clause. 'Let's imagine,' he said, 'that the hope we have in Christ is just for this life.' Let's imagine that Jesus means something only for the realm we can see, the sphere of our mortal senses. What if Christ has significance only for today and not for eternity? What if our hope to live in the bodies God gave us exists only in the present? Where would that leave us? We would be the most pitiable people of all (verse 19).

Those who have no hope in the resurrection of Christ and the resurrection to come are to be pitied because they have a misplaced faith. People who have a Jesus for this life only should be viewed with the greatest compassion. They are pathetic and deluded fools. If Jesus has not been raised, and if there is no hope of a future resurrection, then Paul would counsel you to not make fun of Christians but weep for them.

As Christians, we must demonstrate to the world that we are not pitiable people. Our response to the resurrection must be an unbounded joy in Jesus. Whether we realize it or not, joy and rejoicing play a significant role in our apologetics. Do we want others to believe in the risen Christ? Do we want them to know the hope of everlasting life? We give evidence for that hope when we live with delight in the living Saviour.

The Rev. Lachlan Mackenzie served as a Presbyterian minister in the Scottish Highland town of Lochcarron at the end of the eighteenth and into the early nineteenth century. A brief biography combined with a collection of his sermons is entitled *The Happy Man*. He suffered a stroke in 1818 which put a practical end to his ministry. Though he lay paralyzed he could say to those who visited, 'I am taking a faith's look into heaven.'[1] He knew this life was not all there was. He looked heavenward. He looked homeward. The Rev. Mackenzie passed away on April 20 the following year; and he died the happy man, a man he had described as one who 'loves Christ, and longs for glory.'[2] He died a testimony to the living Lord Jesus.

How do you become the happy man or the happy woman, the happy Christian? It won't happen by make-believe. You can't pretend your troubles away or act as though they don't exist. You can't excuse your

---

[1] *The Happy Man: The Abiding Witness of Lachlan Mackenzie* (Edinburgh: Banner of Truth Trust, 1979), 30.

[2] *Ibid.*, 5.

sins and failures and try to convince others you have your act together. It isn't difficult to see through the thin veneer people often try to lay over their lives. To live the happy life you must live full of the Holy Spirit. You will find the source of true happiness, the source of abiding joy in the living Lord Jesus and the assurance that he is with you no matter what. The exercise of faith and love is the path to joy. The apostle Peter shows the way: 'Though you have not seen him, you love him. Though you do not now see him, you believe in him and rejoice with joy that is inexpressible and filled with glory' (1 Pet. 1:8).

Paul lists for us five devastating consequences if Jesus had not been raised bodily from the tomb. Look at them again: empty, false, futile, lost, pitiable. It would be difficult to imagine five bleaker, more negative terms. In verse 20, however, the apostle turns the entire argument with the resounding declaration,

> But in fact Christ has been raised from the dead!

Because of the resurrection, the empty has become full. What seemed false turns out to be gloriously true. The futile is no longer fruitless but filled with hope. The lost have been saved. And the pitiable turn out to be the happiest of all!

3

CHRIST THE FIRSTFRUITS

1 Corinthians 15:20-28

But in fact Christ has been raised from the dead, the firstfruits of those who have fallen asleep. ²¹ For as by a man came death, by a man has come also the resurrection of the dead. ²² For as in Adam all die, so also in Christ shall all be made alive. ²³ But each in his own order: Christ the firstfruits, then at his coming those who belong to Christ. ²⁴ Then comes the end, when he delivers the kingdom to God the Father after destroying every rule and every authority and power. ²⁵ For he must reign until he has put all his enemies under his feet. ²⁶ The last enemy to be destroyed is death. ²⁷ For 'God has put all things in subjection under his feet.' But when it says, 'all things are put in subjection,' it is plain that he is excepted who put all things in subjection under him. ²⁸ When all things are subjected to him, then the Son himself will also be subjected to him who put all things in subjection under him, that God may be all in all.

SOLOMON wrote, 'For everything there is a season, and a time for every matter under heaven: a time to be born, and a time to die' (Eccles. 3:1, 2). To those statements Paul would add, 'and a time to be raised from the dead!'

In the first two chapters we have seen Paul's masterful treatment of the resurrection in 1 Corinthians 15, the apostle defends the truth of Christ's bodily resurrection (verses 1-11) and spells out the disastrous consequences if Jesus had not been raised from the dead (verses 12-19). In verses 20-28, the timing and sequence of the resurrection are the focus of his attention. God has appointed a time for the dead to be raised, and that will occur when Jesus comes again. That final victory, however, has already begun. Christ inaugurated it by his own resurrection. You and I live in the time between these resurrections. We live in the tension between the 'already' and the 'not yet.'

The New Testament presents us with a programme of history divided into two ages, the present age and the age to come. When Jesus came, lived, died, and rose again, he ushered in the last days, the days when God's promises were fulfilled in him. God's ultimate purpose, the full-flowering of his kingdom, however, has not yet arrived. There is an age to come. Christ gained victory over sin and death by his sacrifice on the cross and testified to that victory by the resurrection, but the full realization of what he achieved will not occur until he returns.

Perhaps an illustration from history can help us understand this distinction between victory secured and victory won. Two dates were decisive for the success of the Allied forces in Europe during World War II. The first date was 6 June 1944, or D-Day, the day the Battle of Normandy began. The second date was 8 May 1945 or VE Day, the date the Allies accepted the surrender of the German army. Though an interval separated these two occasions, the first inevitably led to the second. The victory at Normandy marked the turning point in the war. D-Day ensured the coming of VE Day.[1]

Christ's victory over death guarantees and assures all who trust in him that the day of the believer's resurrection will come. Warfare and triumph are appropriate metaphors to use to describe the believer's hope, but Paul also uses the agricultural image of firstfruits. The firstfruits are the initial sign of the impending harvest. If the crop has borne firstfruits, then there is more fruit to come. That metaphor, mixed with military overtones, stands out in verses 20-28. Christ, the firstfruits from the dead, reigns until he defeats every enemy and subjects everything to God for his glory. Paul

---

[1] Oscar Cullman, *Christ and Time: The Primitive Christian Conception of Time and History.* Translated by Floyd V. Filson (Philadelphia: Westminster Press, 1950), 84.

unpacks this message in three movements. He begins by demonstrating the certainty of the resurrection, he then shows us the order of events, and finally he gives us the details of Jesus' reign.

The certainty of the resurrection

First, Christ, as the firstfruits, guarantees our resurrection. 'But in fact Christ has been raised from the dead.' The opening words of verse 20 serve as Paul's emphatic rebuttal of the implications listed in verses 12-19. In contradistinction to the dire consequences of a still-dead Jesus, Paul boldly proclaims the risen Lord. The resurrection is a fact. It is an historical, verifiable reality. A vast number of eyewitnesses, including Paul himself, confirmed it (see verses 5-8). Of the resurrection, the apostle was absolutely certain. In addition, Paul was also confident that everyone who dies in Christ will also be raised. He based that assurance on two grounds: organic unity and covenantal solidarity. If you are unfamiliar with this terminology, don't let that deter you from reading further. The concepts are not difficult to understand.

First, not only has 'Christ been raised from the dead,' but as the living Lord he has become 'the firstfruits of those who have fallen asleep' (verse 20). The term *firstfruits* has a rich background in the Hebrew Bible. When the Israelites began to reap their harvests, they were to take a sheaf of the first grain (cluster of grapes, etc.) they had gathered to the house of the Lord and present it to him. You can read the instructions for this in Leviticus 23:9-14. The presentation took place on the day after the Sabbath or the first day of the week, the day Christians now call the Lord's Day. The priest would take the sheaf and wave it before God. You may have imagined the priest doing this the way someone might wave a flag back and forth through the air, but that wasn't the direction of the motion. The priest waved the sheaf upward as though he were heaving it into the air. His was a symbolic gesture of offering the harvest to God.

The feast of firstfruits celebrated two significant truths. First, by presenting the sheaves to God, the Israelites consecrated the entire harvest to him.[1] They acknowledged the Lord's grace in providing the crops, and they recognized him as the ultimate owner of the harvest. Second, the firstfruits were just that—the first of the fruits. They were not the entire harvest but a token of it. The firstfruits served, therefore, as a sign of a greater harvest to come.

This Old Testament feast provides the background imagery for Paul's identification of Christ as the firstfruits of those who have fallen asleep. Once again, the apostle used the metaphor of sleep to describe the death of believers. Those who die in Christ 'have fallen asleep' in him (cf. verse 18). Their souls are with God

[1] Morris, *First Corinthians*, 213.

(2 Cor. 5:8), but their bodies slumber, as it were, in the grave awaiting the resurrection day. As the firstfruits, Christ consecrated all of the 'resurrection harvest' to God and guarantees a greater harvest to come. If there are firstfruits, then there will be more fruit! As will become evident in the following verses, Paul uses this imagery to stress the proper order of events with regard to the resurrection. Redemptive history reveals the sequence of Christ's resurrection first, then the resurrection of those who belong to Christ at his coming (verse 23). In addition to this sequential order, however, the imagery of firstfruits also demonstrates the organic unity that exists between Christ and his people. When an Israelite presented a sheaf of wheat at the temple, he did not expect to return home to a harvest of grapes. What he presented as the firstfruits was a small sample of what was to come. The firstfruits and the harvest were organically and inseparably united.[1]

This point is fundamental to Paul's doctrine of the resurrection. He did not teach that the resurrection of believers will merely be like the resurrection of Christ, that something unusual happened to Jesus and something unusual will happen to us. The Saviour's resurrection is the actual beginning of the Christian's

[1] Richard B. Gaffin, Jr, *Resurrection and Redemption: A Study in Paul's Soteriology.* The Student Library (Phillipsburg, NJ: P&R Publishing, 1987), 34.

resurrection. Just as one cannot have firstfruits with-out an entire harvest, neither can Christ Jesus be raised from the dead without his people also being raised up on the last day. Christ's resurrection has an 'all-controlling significance ... for the future of his people'[1] and presents us the strongest possible grounds for confidence and hope. When we ask, 'will we be raised on the last day?' the answer is 'Yes!' because our resurrection has already begun.

In addition to this organic unity between the first-fruits and the harvest, Paul also stresses the covenantal solidarity that exists between Christ and those raised in him. In other words, the assurance of our resurrec-tion not only has a rich background in the symbolism of Israel's worship, it has a theological basis as well. How can the dead be raised? Verse 21 answers that question with a general theological principle: resurrec-tion must come by or through a man the same way death entered the world. Death did not exist as a part of God's original and good creation. Death entered the world through a man, and the curse of death can only be reversed by a man.

Paul works out this principle further in verse 22 where he presents more of the specifics: 'For as in Adam all die, so also in Christ shall all be made alive.' In the creation account (Gen. 1–3), the Lord God gave

---

[1] Herman Ridderbos, *Paul: An Outline of His Theology*. Translated by John Richard de Witt (Grand Rapids: Eerdmans, 1975), 538.

Adam and Eve access to all the trees of the garden of Eden except the tree of the knowledge of good and evil. They were not to eat of that tree upon the pain of death. The Lord told Adam to obey, but he chose to disobey. He ate of the tree and found himself alienated from God because of his disobedience. That alienation was the experience of spiritual death, and from that moment he began to die physically (see Gen. 2:15-17; 3:19). Adam's sin, however, affected more than himself. He was the head of the human race. That was true biologically because we are all descended from him as our first father, but it was also true theologically. Adam stood before God not only as the physical head of humanity but as its covenantal representative as well. His life and actions represented those of his descendants so that when he sinned, we sinned in him. Compare this to what the apostle wrote in Romans 5:12, 'Therefore, just as sin came into the world through one man, and death through sin, and so death spread to all men because all sinned.'

The New England Primer was the first textbook designed for the American Colonies. Published between 1687 and 1690, it became a successful educational tool well into the eighteenth century. To teach the basics of the alphabet, it contained a series of rhymes connected with each letter. It began, of course, with the letter 'A,' and the rhyme was:

> In Adam's fall
> We sinned all.

That simple lesson designed for children sums up Paul's doctrine of original sin and gets right to the heart of his theology. God works on the principle of representation. You may think that isn't fair. After all, you didn't eat from the tree of the knowledge of good and evil. You weren't in the garden that day. Ah, but you were! And so was I! We were in Adam.

When Adam failed as the covenant head of mankind, the Lord sent a second Adam, another representative to live in our place, to obey God for us, and to die and take the penalty for our sin (cf. verse 3). This second Adam is Jesus Christ. Now, if all those in Adam die, and that includes the entire human race, then all those who are in Christ will be made alive.[1] Paul also makes this point in Romans 5:15, 18, 'For if many died through one man's trespass, much more have the grace of God and the free gift by the grace of that one man Jesus Christ abounded for many ... Therefore, as one trespass led to condemnation for all men, so one act of righteousness leads to justification and life for all men.'

---

[1] The adjective 'all' does not stand by itself, isolated from the prepositional phrases in Adam or in Christ. All who are in Adam die. Likewise all who are in Christ, but only those who are in Christ, will be made alive. '[T]here is no dying outside of Adam, there is no quickening apart from Christ. With abstract, absolute universalism this has nothing to do whatsoever.' Geerhardus Vos, *The Pauline Eschatology* (Phillipsburg, NJ: P&R Publishing, 1986), 241.

Adam's fall into sin explains the mess in which we find ourselves in this world. Death and destruction reign because of sin. The good news of Christ offers the only solution for overcoming the sin, death, and devastation that plague us. Adam left us dead and hopeless, but Christ holds out to us both life and hope. The solution to death by a man is life by a man. This, however, is no ordinary man. He is the God-man, the Son of God incarnate, Jesus Christ. The hope of eternal life is found only in him.

The question, then, is whether you are in Adam or in Christ? If you're in Adam, then you are still in your sins. You're still under condemnation. You will not only die physically, but you will also suffer eternal death, eternal separation from God. If you are in Christ, however, then you will be made alive. Your body will be raised on the last day, and you will live forever in the joy and bliss of everlasting life.

If you trust in Christ and are united to him, then the ground of your assurance of salvation and the guarantee of your resurrection isn't found in what you do, in how well you act, in how religious you are, nor in the rituals you perform. The confidence that you will live again and live with God forever is anchored entirely in what Christ has accomplished on your behalf. Too often we base our Christian experience on how we feel. The basis of our hope, however, is what God has done for us in Christ. Only by the objective truth of the gospel can we get our emotions in line with the truth.

Paul combines organic unity with covenantal solidarity to provide the church with an unshakable foundation for assurance in the face of death. Life is uncertain. How long will I live? How will I die? How can I face death with peace and confidence? No one can answer the first two questions, and the only answer for the third is in Christ. The Lord Jesus is the only one who can give us the comfort and peace we need when we have to face the death of a loved one or friend, and he is the only one who can give us courage and hope in the face of our own approaching death. With that confidence, however, we can live boldly for Christ and his kingdom. We need not fear man who can only kill the body (cf. Matt. 10:28) because the resurrection has already begun.

The order of the resurrection

Christ is the firstfruits of the resurrection, and if he is the firstfruits then there are, if you will, 'secondfruits.' In other words, when it comes to the resurrection there is a proper sequence to the events. Yes, all in Christ will be made alive, 'but each in his own order' (verse 23). The term translated *order* in the ESV means *class*, *group*, or *rank*. It only occurs here in the New Testament, but it appears several times in the Septuagint (the Greek translation of the Hebrew Bible), primarily in

Numbers where it describes the order or setting of the tribes of Israel as they camp and march.[1] This term also occurs in military contexts with the sense of 'rank.' Paul's use of it here, however, stresses sequence rather than hierarchy.[2] Verses 23 and 24 spell out the order or arrangement for us: Christ, then those who belong to him, then the end.

Once again, Paul describes Christ as the first-fruits. Jesus is the first, but not because he was the first person raised from the dead. The Old Testament records several resurrections. Elijah raised the widow of Zarephath's son (1 Kings 17:17-24), Elisha raised the son of the Shunammite (2 Kings 4:18-37). Later, when a man's body was thrown into Elisha's grave, the man came back to life (2 Kings 13:20, 21). In addition to these accounts from the Hebrew Bible, the Lord Jesus also raised several people from the dead including the widow of Nain's son (Luke 7:11-17), Jairus' daughter (Luke 8:52-56), and his dear friend Lazarus (John 11:38-44). Jesus was not the first to be raised from the dead, but he was the first one to be raised and never die again. The Shunammite's son eventually died a second time and so too did Lazarus, but as the

---

[1] See Num. 2:2, 3, 10, 18, 25, 31, 34; 10:14, 18, 22, 25.

[2] 'All that Paul teaches is, that, although the resurrection of Christ secures that of his people, the two events are not contemporaneous.' Charles Hodge, *A Commentary on 1 and 2 Corinthians*. A Geneva Series Commentary (1857; Edinburgh: Banner of Truth Trust, reprint 1988), 326.

firstfruits Christ experienced a never-ending victory over death.[1]

Next in the resurrection sequence are those who belong to Christ. They are the remainder of the harvest to be raised. Paul again expresses the key issue of salvation but uses different terms. Earlier he referred to the saved as those who are in Christ. Those who trust in the Lord Jesus are inseparably united to him. They are in union with Christ.[2] In verse 23, he described believers as those who belong to Christ. If you are in Christ, then you are one with him and he is one with you. If you are in Christ, then you belong to him. He has purchased you from the slave market of sin and redeemed you from its bondage so that you might be his (cf. Eph. 1:7). Since all those who are in Christ will be made alive (verse 22), those who belong to Christ will be raised from the dead. Paul thought of the

---

[1] The New Testament sometimes refers to Jesus as the firstborn from the dead (Col. 1:18; Rev. 1:5). 'The fact that Christ is here [Col. 1:18] called the firstborn implies that those who are his brothers and sisters will also arise from the dead, so that, as we learn from Romans 8:29, Christ might be "the firstborn among many brethren." In John 14:19, in fact, Christ specifically says to his disciples, "Because I live, you will live also."' Anthony A. Hoekema, *The Bible and the Future* (Grand Rapids: Eerdmans, 1979), 246.

[2] 'Union with Christ is really the central truth of the whole doctrine of salvation not only in its application but also in its once-for-all accomplishment in the finished work of Christ.' John Murray, *Redemption: Accomplished and Applied*, 165. See pages 165-77 for an excellent treatment of the subject.

believer's salvation in terms of union and ownership, and both are inseparably linked to his or her resurrection.

When will the resurrection occur? At his coming. The word *coming* is a common term in the New Testament for the Lord's second advent. It occurs in secular literature to describe the arrival of a king, and that is what makes it such an appropriate term for Jesus' return. He rules and reigns in heaven (cf. verse 25) and will come again to judge. Christ's second coming is the culmination of his work. Jesus will come again and bring to completion his work of redemption. On that day everyone who belongs to him will be raised to everlasting life.

Then comes the end, the conclusion or termination of fallen human history. From that point onwards, life as we know it will not continue. The end, however, since it follows the resurrection of believers, is also the goal. It is the termination point for which God has been aiming in the salvation of his people. At that point, redemptive history will have reached its climax.

Paul defines the end in verse 24 not only in terms of the saints' resurrection but also in terms of what Christ will do: 'Then comes the end, when he delivers the kingdom to God the Father after destroying every rule and every authority and power.' When the Lord Jesus returns, he will present to his Father the created realm which he has subdued as his kingdom.

The Son will have subdued some people by grace and made them his children. Others he will subjugate by his sovereign power, but through it all he will establish his universal reign. On that day, every knee will bow and every tongue confess that Jesus is Lord (Phil. 2:10, 11). At that point, he will hand over the kingdom to his Father and say, 'Father, I have done this for you. I have accomplished your will.'

Paul further describes the end as occurring after Christ destroys every rule, authority, and power. The term translated *after* is the same word translated *when* earlier in the verse. Christ's delivery of the kingdom to the Father may occur logically after he has destroyed all opposition, but Paul wants his readers to see both of these events as simultaneous descriptions of the end. The end is not only the deliverance of the kingdom to the Father, the end is also the destruction of these powers.

What are these hostile forces? The terms Paul chooses (*rule*, *authority*, and *power*) often refer to the demonic realm. These are spiritual authorities and powers (cf. Eph. 1:21; 3:10; Col. 2:10, 15). At the end Jesus will have fully rendered powerless all the spiritual armies that are arrayed against him. Peter described Christ's ascension as dominion over these powers. The Lord Jesus 'has gone into heaven and is at the right hand of God, with angels, authorities, and powers having been subjected to him'

(1 Pet. 3:22). But surely this victory must include Christ's triumph over all hostile human forces as well.[1] In the end, nothing and no one will stand in opposition to him.

How are these powers destroyed? Will they cease to exist? Is Christ's purpose to annihilate them? The verb the ESV translates *destroy* doesn't mean to abolish or eliminate from existence but to make ineffective or powerless (cf. *put down*, KJV). If someone removed the battery from your car and drained the gasoline from its tank, the car would continue to exist but be completely powerless to get you from one place to the next. By removing the automobile's sources of power, it could no longer function purposefully. Demonic and hostile forces currently fight and rage against the Lord Jesus and his people, but when Christ returns, he will render them ineffective. They will continue to exist in the sufferings of everlasting damnation, but they will be powerless to keep up their warfare against Christ and his church.

Christ's victory reminds us, then, that we should not be intimidated by or despair over the hostile forces we see around us. The apostles were courageous. They entered the major cities of the Roman Empire and preached Jesus as Lord. They knew that Christ, the risen king, possessed all authority over every power in the world. That confidence should also give us courage.

[1] Hodge, *1 and 2 Corinthians*, 330-31.

We should not give up in hopelessness over the way sin seems to have the upper hand. No matter how much wickedness appears to reign in the present, it will not reign forever. Sinful agendas that rule the policies of nations now will not rule endlessly. The persecution of our brothers and sisters in other lands will not continue forever. The church that now seems so weak will not be weak forever. When the Lord Jesus hands over the kingdom to his Father, every wrong will be put right! The hope of the resurrection, therefore, gives the Christian backbone. Believers do not have to be afraid to stand up and speak up for the cause of Christ because the victory belongs to him.

As we look back over verses 23 and 24, we have to ask why this sequence—Christ raised first, then believers at his coming, and then the end—was so important for Paul? I believe it is possible to argue for its significance along several lines. It may have been that some members of the 'no-resurrection' party in Corinth asserted the resurrection was already past. If a person had been saved, then his or her soul had been 'raised' to new life, and that was the only resurrection they could expect. A future, bodily resurrection would not occur. Hymenaeus and Philetus taught this error (2 Tim. 2:17, 18), and it may have had an earlier impact in the church at Corinth as well.[1] On the other hand, Paul

---

[1] F. F. Bruce, *1 and 2 Corinthians.* New Century Bible Commentary (Grand Rapids: Eerdmans, 1971), 144. See also Thomas R.

clearly sees this sequence as another source of comfort for those who questioned what would happen in the future. The bodies of believers will be rescued from their graves before the end. The grave, therefore, is not the end. The Christian's body will not be destroyed when Christ returns and the old heavens and earth are refined through fire and judgment (cf. 2 Pet. 3:10).

This sequence was also a significant part of Paul's apologetic for the resurrection. It would have been easy for those who denied the resurrection to argue their case along these lines: 'You say you believe in the resurrection of the dead. Well, tell me then, have you ever seen anyone raised from the dead? No? Then how can you be so sure it will happen?' To counter this kind of scepticism, the apostle reminded the Corinthians that they should not expect the resurrection until Jesus returns. The fact that Christ had been raised (cf. verses 5-8, 20), however, was all the empirical evidence they needed to be certain that the resurrection had begun. The harvest was underway, and the Son of God would complete it at his second coming.

Christ's reign until the resurrection

Moving on from his discussion of the sequence of events and the ultimate triumph of the kingdom, Paul explains Christ's destruction of all hostile forces and

---

Schreiner, *Paul: Apostle of God's Glory in Christ* (Downers Grove, IL: InterVarsity Press, 2001), 456-57.

his ultimate triumph in verses 25-28. In these verses, he uses two passages from the Psalms and then shows how the Saviour's victory moves inexorably to a supreme purpose, an ultimate goal at the conclusion of all things. Christ, as the firstfruits of the resurrection, not only guarantees our resurrection and establishes the order of the resurrection, he also reigns until the resurrection. Paul's assertion does not argue for the present reign of Jesus in glory; it assumes his reign and asserts its necessity: 'For he must reign until he has put all his enemies under his feet. The last enemy to be destroyed is death' (verses 25, 26).

The seeming problem with Christ's resurrection is that believers still die. Christians grow old, battle disease, are killed in accidents, and sometimes die mysteriously for no apparent reason at all. But they die.[1] The Lord Jesus' resurrection does not free his people from facing death in this world. The effects of sin are powerful and pervasive. We live in a fallen world that groans under the burden of the curse and everyone, including Christians, has to suffer the physical consequences of the curse. Christ's reign at the Father's right hand, however, assures us that death will not be the final word. Christ reigns, and it is necessary that he reign until he puts all of his enemies under his feet. That is, he must occupy his exalted position in heaven as the resurrected Lord putting down enemy

[1] Fee, *First Corinthians*, 752.

after enemy, rendering them ineffective and powerless until he destroys the last one.

Paul opens this last section of the paragraph by quoting from Psalm 110:1, 'The LORD says to my Lord: "Sit at my right hand, until I make your enemies your footstool."' This royal psalm is one of the most often quoted or alluded to Messianic passages in the New Testament. The apostles clearly saw its prophetic import. They interpreted David's words in the light of Christ's ascension and applied this passage to his session at the Father's right hand. Christ Jesus rules and reigns as king. His kingly authority and power are not something that he is waiting to receive in the future; it is something he possesses now. Christ must continue to exercise that power until he defeats all his enemies, including the final one—death itself (verse 26).

Our Saviour's victory over the power of death was achieved at the cross when he underwent the penalty of death on our behalf. His death was the death of death, and his subsequent resurrection gave full and public proof that his triumph on the cross was successful. Death is not finally defeated, however, until the full resurrection harvest comes. But that day will come! Leon Morris wrote, 'At present no man can resist the touch of death. Then death will be able to touch no man.'[1] Death is the enemy. God created us for life, and

[1] Morris, *First Corinthians*, 216-17.

death is the awful intruder, the unwelcome guest that eventually visits every home, but a time is coming when death will be no more. The only way that we can face death now is to know that it is already a defeated foe.

Many years ago I worked with a man named Bill. Bill dearly loved Christ and faithfully served him. Bill encouraged me and counselled me, and he and I became good friends. Not long after I left that job and began to serve as a pastor, I received word that Bill had an inoperable brain tumour. It was cancerous, and he would soon die. My wife and I went to see him and his wife. I was heartbroken, but the entire time we visited them, they exhibited a strong faith in Christ, the faith that his soon-coming death would not be the end. Not long after our visit, Bill sat down with his pastor to plan his funeral. His instructions to the pastor were, 'When you get to the part in the message about death, mock it because it will not win!' Death may touch us for a little while, and barring the second coming of Christ, it will touch us all. But when Jesus returns, it will never touch us again!

Death will be rendered powerless 'For God has put all things in subjection under his feet' (verse 27). Here, with an appeal to Psalm 8:6, Paul presents the reason Christ will destroy even death itself: the Father has put everything under the feet of his Son. Psalm 8 is a song of praise to God for his glory which is above the heavens (verse 1), a glory above the majestic beauty of his celestial creation (verse 3). In light of such surpassing glory, what is man that God would even bother to think about him (verse 4)? Yet, the Lord crowned man with glory and honour and gave him dominion over creation and put all things under his feet (verses 5-8). These verses describe Adam and mankind in general, but they find their ultimate fulfilment in Jesus Christ. If the first Adam was given dominion, how much more the second Adam! The promise of Psalm 8:6 declares that all things will be brought ultimately into subjection to Christ. All rule, authority, power, and death itself will be placed under his feet. He will be victorious over them all.

When Christ returns and places everything in subjection to God the Father, then the Son of God himself will also be in subjection to the Father. Some have read this passage to mean that the Son of God is not as great as or equal with God the Father, but those views hardly do justice to the doctrine of Christ taught elsewhere in the New Testament.[1] The Son of God, in submission to the Father's will, does everything the Father asks, and then hands over his finished work to the Father.

The purpose of this subjection is that 'God may be all in all' (verse 28). Here is the ultimate and over-arching motive for all that God is doing in Christ.

---

[1] The New Testament bears unquestionable testimony to the full deity of the Lord Jesus. See John 1:1; Rom. 9:5; Phil. 2:5-11; Col. 1:15-20; Titus 2:12, 13; Heb. 1:8 as a few notable examples.

The statement that 'God may be all in all' isn't some form of pantheism where God becomes all things and all things become God. It is a statement of his supremacy. Christ has been raised to defeat death and submit everything to his Father so that there will be no more opposition to God's authority, and everyone will honour and worship him!

Where does this passage leave us? It should leave us on our faces before the Almighty in worship and adoration! Do you realize the astonishing implication of Paul's statement? If God's glory is the ultimate goal of Christ's victory, then as you and I live for his glory, we testify to the reality that the age to come has already broken into the present. The way we live and the attitudes we display are not inconsequential. They provide us with the opportunity to say to a watching world, 'Jesus lives and reigns!'

When the farmer harvests his crops, he is well-aware that all the prior hard work was preparation. A farmer's goal isn't ploughing, sowing, watering, or weeding. Those are means to an end. His goal is the harvest because only then is the crop ready for use. Only at harvest time is the wheat ready to make nourishing bread or the grapes ready to make delicious wine. When the harvest day comes, we will realize our lives have been the preparation, the means to a greater end. The goal of God's harvest is that he be celebrated as all in all. Why not start living for that goal today?

4

A RESURRECTION-SHAPED LIFE

1 Corinthians 15:29-34

Otherwise, what do people mean by being baptized on behalf of the dead? If the dead are not raised at all, why are people baptized on their behalf? ³⁰ Why are we in danger every hour? ³¹ I protest, brothers, by my pride in you, which I have in Christ Jesus our Lord, I die every day! ³² What do I gain if, humanly speaking, I fought with beasts at Ephesus? If the dead are not raised, 'Let us eat and drink, for tomorrow we die.' ³³ Do not be deceived: 'Bad company ruins good morals.' ³⁴ Wake up from your drunken stupor, as is right, and do not go on sinning. For some have no knowledge of God. I say this to your shame.

S OME of the special treats available each year at Easter include chocolate bunnies and cream-filled chocolate eggs. Chocolate, of course, does not naturally occur in the shape of either rabbits or eggs. To get those cute and tasty treats, the candy has to be moulded. Liquid chocolate is poured or injected into a form and allowed to harden. Through this process the candy takes on the shape and size of the mould. Once it is removed, it looks like the mould. One quick glance and you know which form the chocolatier used.

Just as a candy mould shapes chocolate, ideas, philosophies, theologies, and value systems shape our lives. They mould the way we think, how we feel, and where we expend our time and energy. When someone looks at your life, when they listen to your conversations or see the way you react to circumstances, what do they see? What mould would they recognize as having shaped you?

Perhaps they see a dollar sign because it is evident you live for material possessions. They may perceive an ego-shaped life since pride has fashioned you into the person you've become. Then again, your life may resemble the ephemeral shapes of the world of entertainment because you live for pleasure. When you look at the people around you, it becomes clear that many moulds are in use. They include bitterness, anger, lust, laziness, and any number of other sins that have such a detrimental impact on the way we live.

What should shape your life? I feel certain that, as a professing Christian, you know the answer is Jesus, but what is it about Jesus specifically in this passage that should have such a significant impact on your life? It is his resurrection and the hope it gives you for your resurrection. When you look back in redemptive history to the victory of Christ over death and then look to the future certainty that you too shall rise, that should change everything about the way you live in the present.

In this next section of 1 Corinthians 15, Paul raises several rhetorical questions. He begins with the startling and oft-debated question, 'If the dead aren't going to be raised, then why do people get baptized for them' (cf. verse 29)? He goes on to ask, 'For that matter, if the dead aren't going to be raised, then why put your life in danger to serve Christ' (cf. verses 30-32). He then concludes with a series of imperatives (verses 33, 34). When you look at these questions and commands in this context, it becomes apparent that the underlying principle that led Paul to raise them is this: the way we live should reveal what we actually believe, and what we believe should have a sanctifying effect on the way we live. Here, then, is the question you ought to ask yourself: am I living a resurrection-shaped life? If you are, then it should be evident in three areas. The first of these is worship.

Resurrection-shaped worship

Paul tightly ties verse 29 to what precedes it with the word *otherwise*. With an emphatic rebuttal of the 'no-resurrection' scenarios of verses 12-19, the apostle unequivocally declares Jesus to be the risen Lord (verses 20-28). He then asks, 'If Christ has not been raised, and the dead will not be raised, then why are people baptized on behalf of the dead?' The apostle raises this issue as a rhetorical question to point out the inconsistency of denying the future resurrection and also being baptized for the dead. He then repeats himself for emphasis: 'If the dead are not raised at all, why are people baptized on their behalf' (verse 29)?

This text is one of the most difficult verses to interpret in the New Testament. Bible scholars and commentators have puzzled over Paul's words for centuries. Some have tried to solve this theological conundrum by reinterpreting or retranslating the basic terms of the statement.[1] Some interpreters attempt to explain the term *baptism* as something other than water baptism. In defence of this view, they appeal

---

[1] In addition to the other commentaries and theologies referred to in the notes for this section, see the survey of various questions and options involved in interpreting this verse in Fee, *First Corinthians*, 763-67.

to passages such as Luke 12:50 where Jesus said, 'I have a baptism to be baptized with, and how great is my distress until it is accomplished!' This 'baptism' referred to his coming suffering and death (cf. Mark 10:38). Does Paul perhaps have that kind of 'baptism' in mind here?

In addition, some exegetes offer an alternate translation for the preposition *on behalf of* and render it *over*. This has led to the creative explanation that some baptisms were held at grave sites. If a believer who had been influential in your conversion passed away, then you might be baptized at his or her grave. Still others interpret the dead in a metaphorical or spiritual way or identify them as a group other than those who had already passed away at the time this letter was written. Are these people who have not yet died, but who are on the verge of death and request baptism?

If one does not find the retranslation and reinterpretation of the key terms acceptable, are there other possible interpretations for this otherwise unknown practice? Indeed there are! New Testament scholars have proposed between thirty and forty different explanations of this text. Let's survey just a few of the major ones. To begin, it is possible that being baptized on behalf of the dead referred to Christians initiated into church roles and offices that were formerly held by believers who had passed away. These people had been baptized, became a part of the visible church, and replaced those who had died. Thus they were baptized on behalf of, or in the place of, the dead. On the other hand, it could mean that some people came to faith in Christ and were baptized because of the influence of a believer who had died. Though the believer had passed away, his or her testimony lived on in the church's memory.[1]

Another proposed solution envisions circumstances in which a person came to faith in Christ but was on the verge of death when he or she requested baptism. Due to severe illness, this person would not be able to live out his or her baptism in a Christian life and were, therefore, baptized for the dead.[2] A variation of this interpretation contends that this practice refers to a person who was converted but, due to age, an accident, disease, or some unexpected reason died before receiving the sacrament of baptism. Another person in the church would then be baptized as a testimony to the deceased individual's faith. Baptism would occur on the dead's behalf but only as a witness borne by another that the departed had died in faith.

We should also consider the possibility that the practice to which Paul refers was an aberrant tradition

[1] Robertson and Plummer, *Critical and Exegetical Comm. 1 Corinthians*, 359-60.

[2] When this person 'saw that death was impending over him, he asked baptism, partly for his own consolation and partly with a view to the edification of his brethren. ... They were, then, baptized for the dead, inasmuch as it could not be of any service to them in this world, and the very occasion of their asking baptism was that they despaired of life.' Calvin, *Comm. 1 Corinthians*, 37.

found only in Corinth. The context makes it clear that false teachers in the church denied the doctrine of the future bodily resurrection of believers. Is it not then also possible that the practice of baptism for the dead was a ritual that these same false teachers promoted? Notice that Paul never endorsed the practice. He never said, 'I taught you to be baptized for the dead.' He may have referred to this practice merely to point out the inconsistency and hypocrisy of the unorthodox party that had infiltrated the church. Why would these false teachers on the one hand deny the future resurrection while on the other hand be baptized for those who had died? It would make no sense at all to be concerned for those who had died if death were the ultimate end.[1]

Having briefly surveyed just a few of the many interpretations of this verse, we might be tempted to throw up our hands and conclude it is impossible to know what Paul meant by this practice. Herman Ridderbos claims, 'The passage is too obscure ... and the materials for comparison too inadequate to reach conclusions that are in any degree well founded.'[2] Is it possible, however, to cut through all of these views

---

[1] As an additional support for this interpretation, one should note the change in subject between verses 29 and 30, 31. Paul first referred to them or to what they were doing: they were being baptized (verse 29). In verse 30, he switched to the first-person plural (and in verse 31 to the first-person singular) to describe what he and the other apostles endured.

[2] Ridderbos, *Paul: An Outline*, 25.

and get to the core of what Paul is talking about? I
believe it is possible if we first clarify what the verse
can't mean and then, second, think about baptism for
the dead in light of what the 'no-resurrection' party
taught.

One of the key principles of biblical interpretation
teaches us to compare Scripture with Scripture and
interpret difficult and obscure passages in the Bible
in the light of passages that are clearer and easier to
understand. When we apply that principle to this
verse, we can say the word of God is clear that water
baptism does not save a person (Titus 3:5; 1 Pet. 3:21,
22). We are justified by faith alone in Christ. Baptism
is the sign and seal of God's covenant of grace, but
water does not wash away our sins. Only the blood
of Jesus Christ shed on the cross can atone for our
iniquity (Eph. 1:7; Heb. 9:11-14; 1 Pet. 1:18, 19). If
water baptism cannot, therefore, save those who are
living, then neither can it save those who die without
Christ. In light of the clear teaching of Scripture,
whatever Paul meant by these words, he cannot mean
that some people were getting baptized for their dead
friends and relatives so that the dead could be released
from hell and allowed into heaven or advance to a
higher level of heaven.[1] That interpretation would

---

[1] The Church of Jesus Christ of Latter-day Saints, commonly
known as the Mormons, teaches that by proxy baptism one can help
advance deceased individuals to a higher state of heaven, though the
deceased must accept this baptism on his or her behalf. 'Because He

fly in the face of a host of straightforward and clear biblical truths.

Next, look at what the expression 'baptized on behalf of the dead' might mean in light of what some in Corinth were teaching. Baptism is water baptism, the sacrament Christ gave to the church. No contextual reason warrants another interpretation. The preposition *on behalf of* means for the sake of. There is no need to look for a different lexical meaning. But who are the dead? If you look at the thrust of Paul's argument, the answer is that the dead is a reference to everyone in Corinth who was baptized and became a part of the church. Paul didn't call them the dead because they were spiritually dead, nor was he merely referring to believers who had already died. He refers to everyone in the church as the dead because everyone will die. Death is the inevitable fact that lies behind the entire discussion in chapter 15. Why would he need to discuss the resurrection at all if not for the fact that everyone must eventually die?

---

is a loving God, the Lord does not damn those people who, through no fault of their own, never had the opportunity for baptism. He has therefore authorized baptisms to be performed by proxy for them. A living person, often a descendant who has become a member of The Church of Jesus Christ of Latter-day Saints, is baptized in behalf of a deceased person. This work is done by Church members in temples throughout the world.' https://www.churchofjesuschrist.org/study/manual/gospel-topics/baptisms-for-the-dead?lang=eng (accessed 29 March 2020). This doctrine not only has no warrant in Scripture, it is contrary to the Bible's doctrine of salvation.

In other words, Paul is saying to the church, 'You are certain to meet death. It is appointed unto everyone once to die (cf. Heb. 9:27). Why, then, identify with Christ's death, burial, and resurrection in baptism if you're going to die and that's it? If there is no future resurrection (verses 20-23), if the last enemy will not be destroyed (verse 26), if all things will not be made subject to the Son of God (verses 27, 28), to identify yourself as a Christian and become a part of the church is a meaningless waste of time!'

The opposite, of course, would also be true. The apostle could well have said, 'If, on the other hand, your faith is rooted in the risen Lord Jesus and you look to the day when you too will be raised, then baptism makes sense. It isn't an empty ritual. Baptism is a means by which God identifies you with the risen Christ and promises that, in him, you too will one day rise from the dead.' When the *Westminster Larger Catechism* defines baptism in question and answer 165, it calls this sacrament '… a sign and seal of ingrafting into [Christ], of remission of sins by his blood, and regeneration by his Spirit; of adoption, and resurrection unto everlasting life …' The symbolism of the sign and the authenticity of the seal are senseless if the resurrection is not a reality.

Can you now see why Paul mentions baptism at this point? To practice baptism in the church and also deny the resurrection of the dead was due either to logical inconsistency, unbelieving hypocrisy, or theological deceit. To be consistent, the 'no-resurrection' party would have to become the 'no-baptism' party as well. What lies beneath the apostle's rhetorical questions in verse 29, then, is an exhortation to theological and ecclesiological consistency. In other words, by raising the question, 'Why don't you preach what you practice?' Paul urged the church to live and worship in light of a firm commitment to the resurrection.

As Christians, our worship in the twenty-first century ought to bear a bright and vibrant testimony to Christ as our risen Lord. We can do that in a number of ways. Clearly, we ought to begin with baptism. While we are not saved by our baptism, we should not neglect this sacrament or treat it as unimportant. Paul's emphasis on his ministry of evangelism in 1 Corinthians 1:13-17 has led some to conclude that baptism is a secondary and inconsequential issue, but this was hardly the apostle's attitude. For Paul, the sacrament of baptism identifies us with the Lord Jesus in his death, burial, and resurrection and challenges us to 'walk in newness of life' (cf. Rom. 6:1-4). A baptized person should not, therefore, live under the power of sin and death but increasingly gain victory in his or her fight against temptation. As Christians, we strive to live out the implications of our baptism when we meditate on and believe in the truth symbolized by this ordinance. We then draw 'strength from the death and resurrection of Christ, into whom we are baptized, for the mortifying of sin, and quickening of grace' (*Westminster Larger Catechism*, 167).

Furthermore, if we believe in the gospel promises of new life given to us in baptism, then Christian parents should baptize their children. God always gave a sign and seal to accompany his covenants. No divine covenant ever stands alone unaccompanied by a sign, and the new covenant is no exception. Just as the covenant promise and seal belonged to Abraham and his offspring, so too does the promise and sign of the new covenant belong to believers and their children (see, e.g., Acts 2:37-39). Abraham circumcised his children, and Christian parents ought to baptize theirs (cf. Col. 2:11, 12).

The resurrection should not only shape our lives with regard to baptism and its meaning and significance, it should frame our attitude toward the Lord's Day as well. As believers in the era of the new covenant, we obey the fourth commandment by observing the Sabbath on the first day of the week. The New Testament did not change the commandment, but it did shift its observance from the seventh day to the first in recognition of Christ's resurrection and its import for the life of the church (see Matt. 28:1; Mark 16:2; Acts 20:7; 1 Cor. 16:2).[1] As a result, Christians began

---

[1] See A. A. Hodge, *The Day Changed and the Sabbath Preserved* (1877).

to refer to their Sabbath as the Lord's Day (see Rev. 1:10). While churches may have special Easter celebrations on the first Sunday after Passover, every Sunday is resurrection Sunday, every Sunday is the Lord's Day. The day belongs to him. He claimed it when he rose from the dead. When we observe the Lord's Day, we testify to the historical reality of Christ's resurrection as well as his lordship over time. If he is Lord over time, then he claims sovereignty over our time as well and sets apart one entire day for himself. We should, therefore, set it apart for him as a day of worship and celebration. It isn't my day or your day or sports day; it is the Lord's Day and his alone.

If the Lord's Day is a resurrection celebration, then our worship must not be perfunctory but thoughtful, theological, joyful, and exuberant. I have seen some Christians sing about Christ's victory and, though the hymn was very orthodox, they looked as though they had just lost their best friend. How can we worship the risen Lord Jesus with long faces? Yes, we must mourn our sin and unfaithfulness. Certainly our unbelief should break our hearts. But if Christ is alive and interceding for us (Heb. 7:25), then we have every reason to hope. We have every reason to smile through our tears of repentance and shout Hallelujah!

Resurrection-shaped risks

Having demonstrated how the resurrection shapes our worship, Paul turns next to ask about the dangers he and others faced. If the dead are not raised, then why would anyone be willing to endure what these people had to endure? A resurrection-shaped life should be evident in the risks one takes.

In verse 30 the apostle writes, 'Why are we in danger every hour?' Who are the *we* with whom Paul associates himself? Several references to *we* occur earlier in the chapter and include 'we preach,' verse 11; 'we are false witnesses' (if the resurrection isn't true), verse 15; 'we testified,' verse 15; and 'we have hope,' verse 19 (cf. our preaching, verse 14). In each case, the pronoun refers to the apostles and witnesses of Christ's resurrection who carried on a ministry of proclamation. In general, the *we* references are to the apostolate.

Paul and all of the apostles were in constant danger from the Romans because they followed Christ and proclaimed him, rather than Caesar, as king and Lord. They were in danger from the Jews as well because their opponents saw them as heretics attempting to overthrow the ancient Jewish faith and way of life. Paul's rhetorical question, 'Why are we in danger?' like the rhetorical questions in verse 29, has the force of a strong assertion. If there is no resurrection, then we are in danger every hour for no good reason.

Though Paul clearly included himself in the *we* of verse 30, he went on in verses 31 and 32 to give a personal example of the danger he had faced. With phraseology similar to a solemn oath, he affirmed that he died daily. 'I protest, brothers, by my pride in you, which I have in Christ Jesus our Lord, I die every day' (verse 31)! How should we read this affirmation? Surely, he didn't expect his readers to take him literally. No one can physically die every day. Perhaps he meant this in a spiritual sense. He exhorted believers to mortify their sins and temptations, to consider themselves to be dead to sin and alive to God. This is the thrust of Romans 6 and 7. This death to sin and self was and is the very demand of Christ for his disciples. The Christian must take up his or her cross and die daily (see Mark 8:34-38). This, no doubt was Paul's practice as well. He grew in grace as he died to self, and he died to self every day.

Given the context of this statement, however, it seems Paul means for his readers to take him more literally than we might initially think. Paul faced hazards, including the risk of losing his life, on a regular basis. Second Corinthians bears an eloquent testimony to the life-threatening hardships he encountered. The apostle wrote, 'For we do not want you to be unaware, brothers, of the affliction we experienced in Asia. For we were so utterly burdened beyond our strength that we despaired of life itself.

Indeed, we felt that we had received the sentence of death. But that was to make us rely not on ourselves but on God who raises the dead' (2 Cor. 1:8, 9). Later, Paul reminds us that he willingly faced hardships and hazards for the sake of his Saviour: 'always carrying in the body the death of Jesus, so that the life of Jesus may also be manifested in our bodies. For we who live are always being given over to death for Jesus' sake, so that the life of Jesus also may be manifested in our mortal flesh. So death is at work in us, but life in you' (2 Cor. 4:10-12). Finally, in chapter 11, he catalogued some of his perils. They included the following: 'Five times I received at the hands of the Jews the forty lashes less one. Three times I was beaten with rods. Once I was stoned. Three times I was shipwrecked; a night and a day I was adrift at sea; on frequent journeys, in danger from rivers, danger from robbers, danger from my own people, danger from Gentiles, danger in the city, danger in the wilderness, danger at sea, danger from false brothers; in toil and hardship, through many a sleepless night, in hunger and thirst, often without food, in cold and exposure' (2 Cor. 11:24-27).

If Paul faced the possibility of death every day, and faced it from a multitude of directions, then every day he had to die to self and be willing to face the prospect of his demise for the gospel. Do you know anything of that kind of surrender to God? Have you learned to place your life in the Lord's hands each day to be used in life, or in death, as he sees fit?

Verse 31 paints the perils of first-century ministry with broad strokes, but verse 32 is specific: 'What do I gain if, humanly speaking, I fought with beasts at Ephesus?' Paul wrote this letter from Ephesus. He had ministered in that city for three years and now, near the end of his time there, he reflects on the hardships he had faced. As a Roman citizen, it would have been unlikely that Paul would have been thrown into the arena to face lions. And even if his citizenship had been violated and he was forced to endure such an ordeal, it would have been unlikely for him to survive.[1]

But humanly speaking, Paul did fight with beasts at Ephesus. Unbelievers opposed his preaching, and he faced demonic forces (Acts 19:11-20). When the manufacturers of idols started to lose business because of the gospel's impact in the city, a riot erupted and Paul's friends kept him from entering the fray lest he be torn limb from limb (Acts 19:21-41). Yes, he faced 'wild beasts' at Ephesus.

The question, however, is *Why?* Why would Paul and his fellow apostles risk all of the dangers, hardships, and losses related to preaching the gospel if this life is all there is and they had no resurrection hope?

The force of the logic is not lost on Paul, and he points out the absurdity of it all with the concluding

---

[1] Fee, *First Corinthians*, 770-71; Bruce, *1 and 2 Corinthians*, 149-50.

words of verse 32: 'If the dead are not raised, "Let us eat and drink, for tomorrow we die."' Here Paul quotes Isaiah 22:13. Understanding the context of that chapter helps us to understand why he chose to use those words in this situation. The prophet Isaiah foretold with great pathos the coming destruction of Jerusalem (22:1-8a). The Israelites were diligent to fortify the city against enemy attack, but they were unmindful of God (22:8b-11). They were militarily savvy but spiritually foolish. The Lord called them to repent, but they chose to party. Rather than repent, they revelled. They pursued pleasure, heedless to God's call and careless of spiritual things (22:12-14). Their mantra was 'Let us eat and drink, for tomorrow we die' (22:13b).

Paul saw this attitude of inattention to spiritual reality and the pursuit of the immediate, to be the logical position of anyone who denied a future resurrection. Why put your life on the line? Why face dangers for the gospel if you die and that's it? If the dead will not rise from their graves, then risky ministry is absurd. But if Christ has been raised and if the dead will be raised, then nothing is too much for Jesus to ask from us.

Have you ever taken a risk? Perhaps you started a business or invested in a new company. You may have taken some risks when you decided to take up a new sport. It may have seemed like a huge risk when you asked that cute girl, 'Would you like to go out on a date?' The risk in those, and numerous other scenarios, is that we may not receive in return what we hoped for. We may lose our money in the investment. That new sport may injure our bodies rather than help us become more fit. That certain someone may turn down our offer for dinner with a flimsy excuse that really says, 'No, and don't ask again.'

No one can serve the Lord Jesus without taking risks. No, you don't have to face lions in a Roman arena, and you may not be thrown in jail for giving someone a gospel tract, but you will have to face the risk of being rejected, hurt by harsh words, made fun of, overlooked for promotions, or banished from family gatherings. Risk is real, but the return we hope for is absolutely certain because the dead will be raised.

Several pastors and I often send text messages to each other on Sunday morning. Most of the time these are notes to let each other know that we're praying for one another as we preach. Often these texts will include a Bible verse or some word of encouragement. Recently, one of my friends sent a line from Esther Rushthoi's gospel song. It read simply, 'It will be worth it all when we see Jesus.'

Will you take up your cross? Will you die to self? Will you surrender to serve Christ and embrace the risks, whatever they may be, to follow him? If you will, then on the day of resurrection you will say, 'It was worth it all!'

Resurrection-shaped holiness

The third and final area Paul highlights is the believer's quest for godly living. A resurrection-shaped life should be evident in the holiness you pursue. Much of what Paul wrote in verses 29-32 is couched in the form of rhetorical questions. In the final two verses of this paragraph, however, he switches to the mode of command. Three imperatives set forth the apostolic agenda for godliness. 'Do not be deceived: "Bad company ruins good morals." Wake up from your drunken stupor, as is right, and do not go on sinning. For some have no knowledge of God. I say this to your shame' (verses 33, 34).

As with so many issues in this letter, Paul attempts to correct a problem in the church. He, therefore, did not want the Corinthians to be tricked or deceived into thinking a denial of the future resurrection was an acceptable position to maintain.

To make his point, Paul inserts a second quotation. Unlike the words from Isaiah in verse 32, here he introduces a proverb from the secular author Menander. This aphorism comes from Menander's lost comedy *Thais*, 'Bad company ruins good morals.'[1] Benjamin Franklin restated the maxim this way, 'He that lieth down with dogs shall rise up with fleas.' The people

---

[1] Norman Hillyer, '1 and 2 Corinthians' in *The New Bible Commentary: Revised*. Edited by D. Guthrie and J. A. Motyer (Grand Rapids: Eerdmans, 1970), 1072.

with whom you associate have a greater influence on your life than you often realize. Parents know this, and it is the reason they carefully choose their children's playmates. If we spend time with people who are morally debased, dishonest, or greedy, their influence will start to rub off on us.

This same principle applies to ideas. The thoughts and concepts that bombard us each day can, if we are not very careful, have a huge negative impact on our doctrine and, consequently, our growth in godliness. Paul did not want the Corinthians to be tricked into thinking false teachers who denied the resurrection would have no deleterious effect on the church and its ministry. Doctrine matters. What we think and what we believe influences the way we live.

One of the clearest illustrations of this point is the theological and moral decline in many of the mainline denominations. My own theological tradition has its roots in Southern Presbyterianism. The Presbyterian Church US witnessed a weakening and compromise in its theology over several decades until many in the church taught and endorsed liberal and unorthodox doctrine.[1] After 1983, when the PCUS joined with the United Presbyterian Church to form the Presbyterian Church (USA), the theological and moral decline

[1] This decline led to the formation of the Presbyterian Church in America in 1973. See the historical record in Sean Michael Lucas, *For a Continuing Church: The Roots of the Presbyterian Church in America* (Phillipsburg, NJ: P&R Publishing, 2015).

continued. The decay has now reached the lamenta-
ble point where the denomination officially endorses
unbiblical sexual behaviour and views abortion as a
legitimate, individual choice. Ungodly doctrine has
led to ungodly conduct. Do not be deceived!

Next, Paul commands the Corinthians to wake up.
As long as they continued to tolerate the 'no-resurrection'
party in the church and failed to recognize the implications and deadly effects of false doctrine, it was as
though they were in a stupor. To wake up was the right
thing to do.

Furthermore, they must not go on sinning. This
third imperative is, on the one hand, a general call to
holiness. They should repent of any and every sin. In
the context, however, Paul's specific target is the sin
of tolerating unbelief. To allow false teachers in their
midst and to question cardinal doctrines of the faith
was a sin which must stop. Theological compromise on
the core issues of Christianity is a sin against God. It
dishonours the Lord Jesus Christ and brings his glorious name into disrepute. Yes, a stand for the truth may
lead to people insulting you and calling you narrow-
minded, but that is a risk for the gospel you must take.
The Lord is more interested in your holiness and the
church's purity than in so-called open-mindedness and
the world's approval.

Paul concludes, 'For some have no knowledge
of God. I say this to your shame' (verse 34b). The

Corinthians need to wake up to the fact that just because people associated themselves with the church that didn't mean they are actually saved or knew the Lord. Some who were part of the visible church quite obviously did not know Christ, and that was to the Corinthians' shame. They ought to feel the embarrassment for having allowed unsaved people into positions of leadership or at least allowing them significant influence in the church where they had spread their destructive doctrines. Paul could expect better from this church. They were equipped with Scripture and the Holy Spirit. Spiritual growth and progress toward Christian maturity should have been taking place so that at least the leaders in the church could deal with these issues. They should have been ashamed because they had not recognized the doctrinal sin as well as the moral deviations associated with it and dealt decisively with them. Would Paul say similar things to our shame as well?

What does your life look like? What is shaping you and making you into the person you're becoming? Is your life one of worship? Are you willing to take risks for the gospel? Are you pursuing godliness? If not, then why not? What needs to change for you to live a resurrection-shaped life?

5

SOWN AND RAISED: THE RESURRECTION BODY

1 CORINTHIANS 15:35-49

³⁵ But someone will ask, 'How are the dead raised? With what kind of body do they come?' ³⁶ You foolish person! What you sow does not come to life unless it dies. ³⁷ And what you sow is not the body that is to be, but a bare kernel, perhaps of wheat or of some other grain. ³⁸ But God gives it a body as he has chosen, and to each kind of seed its own body. ³⁹ For not all flesh is the same, but there is one kind for humans, another for animals, another for birds, and another for fish. ⁴⁰ There are heavenly bodies and earthly bodies, but the glory of the heavenly is of one kind, and the glory of the earthly is of another. ⁴¹ There is one glory of the sun, and another glory of the moon, and another glory of the stars; for star differs from star in glory.

⁴² So is it with the resurrection of the dead. What is sown is perishable; what is raised is imperishable.

[43] It is sown in dishonor; it is raised in glory. It is sown in weakness; it is raised in power. [44] It is sown a natural body; it is raised a spiritual body. If there is a natural body, there is also a spiritual body. [45] Thus it is written, 'The first man Adam became a living being'; the last Adam became a life-giving spirit. [46] But it is not the spiritual that is first but the natural, and then the spiritual. [47] The first man was from the earth, a man of dust; the second man is from heaven. [48] As was the man of dust, so also are those who are of the dust, and as is the man of heaven, so also are those who are of heaven. [49] Just as we have borne the image of the man of dust, we shall also bear the image of the man of heaven.

Y wife and I knew a little boy who, like many children, was intensely curious. His head was filled with questions. He asked *Why?* about everything. One day, after he had posed what seemed to be hundreds of questions, I said to him, 'Okay, enough! No more questions!' To which he responded, 'Why?'

Curiosity can be a very good thing. Professors have discovered that curious students often excel more intelligent students. It turns out that C. Q. (curiosity quotient) can be more fruitful than I. Q. Curiosity leads us to probe, investigate, and ponder. I suppose many people, certainly many Christians, are more curious about the future and the last great events of human history than almost anything else. We want to know when Christ will return. We're eager to know what that day will be like, and which events will precede others leading up to the Saviour's second coming. This curiosity is also deeply personal. We want to know what our lives will be like in the new heavens and new earth. We find it difficult to imagine something other than life as we have experienced it with our weaknesses, imperfections, and sins.

Questions about the future can, however, arise from scepticism. Peter reminds us that scoffers ask about the future when they mock the Lord and say, 'Where is the promise of his coming' (2 Pet. 3:4)? Sin and unbelief often lead scorners to deliberately overlook the fact of God's power (2 Pet. 3:5). In the final analysis, the will, or an unwillingness to believe, typically drives scoffing and scepticism more than the intellect, or an absence of reasons to believe. If C. Q. can outperform I. Q., then S. Q. (scepticism quotient) can undermine both.

Scepticism and unbelief were hard at work in Corinth attempting to subvert the faith of the church. While it is difficult to nail down with precision the exact form the 'no-resurrection' doctrine took, Paul's response in 1 Corinthians 15 clearly indicates that some faction in the church taught there would be no future bodily resurrection of believers. People die, and though their souls continue to exist, their bodies experience corruption in the grave, and disintegration is their final end.

In the previous chapters, we've seen Paul hard at work to counteract this heresy and to point out its inconsistency with the gospel. If one placed his or her faith in the Lord Jesus Christ, the one who died for our sins, was buried, and rose again (verses 3, 4), then how could that same person conclude that believers would not rise from the dead in the future (verses 12-19)? To believe in the resurrection of Christ is to believe in the resurrection of his people because Jesus' resurrection is the firstfruits of the final harvest (verses 20-28). Otherwise, the practice of the church and the risks involved in serving the Lord are all a waste of time (verses 29-34).

After establishing and defending the doctrine of the future resurrection, Paul addresses the question of the sceptic (verse 35). He imagines (or he had heard?) that someone would respond, 'Okay, if you're so smart, if the dead will rise again, then tell me what kind of body will they have?'

Though scepticism is the driving force behind this question, Paul felt it was important to answer it. His answer in verses 35-49 involves a complex argument, but for the apostle, the bottom line is this: On the day of resurrection, the Holy Spirit will transform our bodies to be like Christ's resurrected body. How do we know this? How can we be sure such an amazing transformation will occur? What can silence the scoffing of the sceptic? Paul employs two lines of argument that assure us of this crucial truth: creation and Scripture.

Creation

Was Paul's interlocutor, the 'someone' of verse 35, a theoretical opponent or had an individual or individuals in Corinth raised the issue of the resurrection body, its nature, and its appearance? We can't answer that question with absolute certainty, though it seems likely that the apostle posits the questions found here because he knew they were topics of debate within the church. What we do know is that the questions he raises drive us to the heart of the issue.

The first question, 'How are the dead raised?' focuses on the mechanics of the resurrection. How does a dead body actually come back to life? The second question, 'With what kind of body do they come?' asks about the nature of human existence after the human body has decomposed and been revivified. Both questions are important, and Paul will answer them. He saw, however, that though these questions were significant and needed thoughtful responses, the 'no-resurrection' teachers in Corinth raised them as a means of defending their anti-supernaturalism. That becomes evident in his sharp retort, 'You foolish person' (verse 36)![1] Why did Paul reply in such a brusque way? Because a sceptic who would raise questions like these had failed to open his eyes and observe the most basic features of creation.

At this point, Paul turns his attention to facets of the created order (verses 36b-41) to illustrate the points he will make later in verses 42-49. God reveals himself in creation (see Psa. 19:1-6; Rom. 1:19-23), and from this revelation the apostle draws several helpful analogies. The first analogies or illustrations focus on the plant and animal kingdoms. The people of Corinth were city folks, but Paul expected them to have a basic conception of farming. 'What you sow does not come

[1] Bruce, *1 and 2 Corinthians*, 151.

to life unless it dies. And what you sow is not the body that is to be, but a bare kernel, perhaps of wheat or of some other grain. But God gives it a body as he has chosen, and to each kind of seed its own body' (verses 36-38).

When the farmer sows grain, he sows bare kernels. The kernels that fall to the ground are dry and, for all appearances, dead. They have no semblance of life at all. The grain does, however, sprout and grow. The apparent death of the kernel proves to be no obstacle to new life. The farmer may sow wheat or some other grain, but what he sows looks far different from the plant that springs up from the ground. Gardeners observe this principle on a regular basis. Whether they grow flowers for decorating or vegetables for eating, they know the plant that is produced will be far different from the seed sown. Indeed, it will be far more glorious than the seed!¹

The difference between the seed and the full-grown plant exists because of the will of God (verse 38). The shape, size, colour, and other distinctive features of the plant are all subject to his choice. He gives to each the design he wishes. Paul introduces providential design at this point because it was important not to allow his nature analogy to be twisted or to degenerate into naturalism. God is at work in all the facets of his created order. The underlying point is this:

¹ Morris, *First Corinthians*, 224.

the resurrection body will be different than the body 'sown' in the earth. Just like seed, it will sprout up to new life, resurrection life, according to God's sovereign purpose and plan. Death will prove no obstacle on the last day, and the resurrection body will take the form the Lord has chosen.

Not only does God give to each plant the 'body' that he chooses, those who possess bodies of flesh differ as well. First, Paul makes a general statement, 'For not all flesh is the same' (verse 39), then he expands on that principle. People have human flesh, the beasts of the field have animal flesh. Fowl have the flesh of birds, and fish have their own, unique fishy flesh. Humans do not look like birds. Mammals do not look like fish. You can easily distinguish one from the other. This second nature analogy reminds us that God has designed creation with variety. If we see such a vast array of species in the animal kingdom, then we should not be surprised that variety exists in the realm of the supernatural as well.

Next, in verses 40, 41, Paul turns the gaze of his readers towards heaven. One not only observes variety and distinction in the plant and animal kingdoms, he or she can see it in the cosmological realm as well. 'There are heavenly bodies and earthly bodies, but the glory of the heavenly is of one kind, and the glory of the earthly is of another. There is one glory of the sun, and another glory of the moon, and another glory of the stars; for star differs from star in glory' (verses 40, 41).

A clear distinction exists between earthly bodies, like plants, humans, and animals, and heavenly bodies, like the sun, moon, and stars. A difference in glory exists between them as well. Fields of grain have a splendour to them as do baskets of flowers. We can admire the beauty of a horse or the magnificence of an eagle in flight. We can look into the night sky and be overawed by millions of twinkling stars or experience a sense of calm as we admire a sunset. We can appreciate all of these aspects of creation, but we instinctively recognize that when we say, 'How glorious!' we mean the statement in different ways. Furthermore, even among the heavenly bodies a difference in glory, or at least in degree of glory, occurs as well. One doesn't need a powerful telescope to detect the difference between the blazing light of the noonday sun and the luminescent glow reflected by the moon.

Wherever Paul looked, whether it was up into the sky filled with its stars and planets, down at the ground where the farmer plants his crops, or all around at the variety of people and animals that inhabit the world, he saw the beauty of God's differentiating choice.[1] If God's creative plan for this world includes such a vast array of creatures and such an extensive variety of plants, then why should anyone think that life as we

[1] Morris, *First Corinthians*, 226.

know it in our present bodies is the only kind of bodily existence that there can be or will be?[1]

Scripture

While nature provides Paul with analogies to explain the transformation of the resurrection body, he grounds his entire hope for this change in Scripture itself. In verses 42-49, the apostle moves from the illustrative help he found in general revelation to the authority of special revelation. In the final eight verses of this passage, Paul weaves a tightly knit argument. To understand his line of reasoning, you need first to move through the text and follow his thought one step at a time. Then step back and look at the larger picture in order to see his big ideas.

Having illustrated the transformations, differences, and varying degrees of glory that occur in nature, Paul links his examples to the subject at hand—'So is it with the resurrection of the dead' (verse 42). A change, a transformation will occur. The apostle reverts to his illustration of grain in verses 36, 37, where he picks up the key verb 'to sow.' Just as the farmer sows seed and the seed is transformed, so too will the body 'sown' in the earth be raised and transformed. He then describes this great change in terms of polar opposites. 'What is sown is perishable; what is raised is imperishable. It is sown in dishonor; it is raised in glory. It is sown

[1] Bruce, *1 and 2 Corinthians*, 151.

in weakness; it is raised in power. It is sown a natural body; it is raised a spiritual body' (verses 42-44).

The perishable body is subject to corruptibility, decomposition, and decay. Elsewhere Paul refers to the human body as an earthen vessel or a jar of clay (2 Cor. 4:7). It is fragile, delicate, and easily broken. We experience this fragility in illness and the process of ageing. When we get sick or grow older, our bodies remind us they will not last forever. 'Our outer self is wasting away' (2 Cor. 4:16). Our bodies continue to waste away until they die, and after they die, they decompose. God reminded Adam, 'By the sweat of your face you shall eat bread, till you return to the ground, for out of it you were taken; for you are dust, and to dust you shall return' (Gen. 3:19).

The Christian burial service echoes the solemnity of the Lord's words when over the casket the minister says, 'Forasmuch as it hath pleased Almighty God of his great mercy to take unto himself the soul of our dear brother/sister here departed, we therefore commit his body to the ground; earth to earth, ashes to ashes, dust to dust.'[1] All of us are dust headed to dust.

Though the body is perishable and sown in corruption, it will be raised imperishable. When God raises us

---

[1] Originally composed by Martin Bucer, these words of committal were incorporated into the Anglican *Book of Common Prayer* (1552), and altered in *The Presbyterian Book of Common Prayer* (1864). Terry L. Johnson, Ed., *Leading in Worship*. Revised and Expanded Edition (Powder Springs, GA: Tolle Lege Press, 2013), 331.

from the dead, we will have a body, a physical, human body but a different kind of body. The resurrection body will not be subject to death and decay. Resurrection bodies will be incorruptible and immortal. We don't know the details of what life will be like in the new heavens and the new earth. Will people still work as farmers and engineers? Will we manufacture cars and computers? I'm not sure what life beyond the final great day holds as far as occupations are concerned, except for this—I am certain the day of resurrection will bankrupt every hospital and mortuary in existence!

Paul continues with his descriptions. The body is sown or buried 'in dishonor.' This expression seems a strange choice for the apostle. After all, burial is a way to honour the dead. In what way is the body sown in dishonour? The term *dishonour* means disgrace or shame. The body is buried in dishonour or humiliation because death is the result of sin and God's curse. The shame and disgrace is that death exists at all.

But the dishonour of death will not reign forever. If you are a believer, your body will be raised in glory! Splendour, beauty, and everlasting perfection await those who are in Christ. This thought was uppermost in Paul's mind when he wrote his prison epistles. He reminded the Philippians, 'But our citizenship is in heaven, and from it we await a Saviour, the Lord Jesus Christ, who will transform our lowly body to be like his glorious body, by the power that enables him even to subject all things to himself' (Phil. 3:20, 21). What more encouraging words could he pen than these he wrote to the church in Colossae, 'When Christ who is your life appears, then you also will appear with him in glory' (Col. 3:4)?

Furthermore, our bodies will be sown in weakness. If our bodies are 'sown' when they are buried, then weakness is a suitable term. Weakness characterizes our entire human existence. We've already noted in verse 42 that our bodies are subject to disease and ultimately to decay, and we feel our lack of strength throughout our lives. Isaiah wrote, 'Even youths shall faint and be weary, and young men shall fall exhausted' (Isa. 40:30). Weakness means limitations, inabilities, and feebleness.

Power, however, will characterize our resurrection bodies. Our new bodies will exemplify strength and ability. Never again will they bow down under the weight of our present limitations and failures. Never again will the urge to indulge our flesh with sin defeat us. Our bodies will forever be revived with all the vitality necessary to love, serve, and praise God for all eternity.

What do you look forward to most in the resurrection life to come? We long for the day when we will never again be tired, nor weep, nor lie awake at night burdened with worry. In the new creation, we will never have a friend turn his back on us or a spouse walk away from us. The prospect of no more illness, death, heartache, and loss makes us long for that day. But there is more!

Dr John Gerstner was one of the leading Presbyterian and Reformed theologians of the twentieth century. When my wife and I attended the dedication of the Gerstner Collection, an archive of his books and papers at Geneva College, we had the opportunity to hear his pastor speak at the ceremony. He described Dr Gerstner's last days as he suffered from terminal cancer. At one point he asked Dr Gerstner what he looked forward to most in heaven. He replied, 'I look forward to loving and worshipping God unhindered by sin.' Not only will every Christian be able to do that when his or her spirit is absent from the body and with the Lord (see 2 Cor. 5:8), but one day the Lord will raise us in power and with body and soul we will love and worship and serve him in the power of life, everlasting life unhindered by sin.

The final pair of contrasting descriptions are general and encompass the previous one. 'It is sown a natural body; it is raised a spiritual body' (verse 44). This statement, however, raises the question, 'What is a spiritual body?' Clearly it is a changed body, a body that is imperishable, glorious, and powerful. But why did Paul call it *spiritual*, and what accounts for this transformation? Why is this change going to occur, and how can Paul be so certain it will happen? The apostle bases his argument on Scripture, in particular on the redemptive-historical pattern of the first and last Adam.

At the end of verse 44, Paul takes the fourth contrasting pair of transformations, *natural* and *spiritual*, and develops his argument further. Couched in the logic of an 'if-then' statement, Paul deduces that if a natural body existed, then so too does a spiritual one. No one doubted the existence of the natural body. That people have flesh and blood, that they die and decay, was the underlying assumption of this entire treatise on the resurrection. No one in Corinth, or anywhere else for that matter, needed much convincing of that fact.

What must have startled Paul's readers in Corinth, just as it surprises readers today, is his second assertion—'there is also a spiritual body.' What is a spiritual body, and why is it the corollary to the natural body? The answer comes from the creation of Adam and the pattern Paul saw so clearly entailed in it.

With the words 'Thus it is written,' Paul makes a direct appeal to Scripture and quotes from Genesis 2, 'then the LORD God formed the man of dust from the ground and breathed into his nostrils the breath of life, and the man became a living creature' (Gen. 2:7). When the Lord created Adam, man became a living being with a natural body.

The apostle doesn't stop there, however. He goes on to posit a further statement. If there is a first Adam with a natural body, then there is a last Adam with a spiritual body. This last Adam is 'a life-giving spirit' (verse 45). Following on from his earlier statements in verses 21, 22 and his parallel line of reasoning in Romans 5:12-21, the last Adam is clearly the Lord Jesus Christ. Though only the first half of verse 45 contains a direct quotation from Scripture, all of the verse falls under the rubric of 'thus it is written' because Paul accurately deduced the latter half from what the Scriptures teach.[1]

Paul sees in the Bible a divinely designed pattern in which Adam and Christ stand as the representatives or covenant heads of two peoples.[2] Adam was the head of all humanity, and mankind fell into sin in him (see verses 21a and 22a). Christ, on the other hand, is the covenant head of all those chosen in him, and in him they are made alive (verses 21b and 22b).

Let's see if we can put all of these pieces together to form a simple and clear picture.

[1] 'The whole counsel of God concerning all things necessary for his own glory, man's salvation, faith and life, is either expressly set down in Scripture, or by good and necessary consequence may be deduced from Scripture: unto which nothing at any time is to be added, whether by new revelations of the Spirit, or traditions of men.' *Westminster Confession of Faith*, 1.6 (Edinburgh: Banner of Truth Trust, 2018), 3.

[2] The term *federal head* often occurs in theological literature. This title comes from the Latin noun *foedus* which means covenant.

First, God created Adam a living being with a natural body. Adam fell into sin, and under the effects of sin and the curse, the natural body suffers weakness and dishonour. It dies and perishes. It is buried and experiences corruption.

Second, on the day of resurrection, the natural body that suffered such weakness and decay will be raised a spiritual body. But what exactly is a spiritual body? Is it an ethereal, shapeless, ghost-like appearance without physical properties? Are those raised on the last day meant to float around for all eternity in an insubstantial existence? That can't be Paul's meaning because throughout this entire discourse his emphasis has been on bodily resurrection. Furthermore, based on the seed analogy in verses 35-38, an organic relationship exists between the physical body 'sown' in the grave and the body raised by God.

Throughout his letters Paul uses the adjective *spiritual*, to describe the work of the Holy Spirit. The only exception to this rule is its use in Ephesians 6:12 where the context unmistakably indicates the reference is to demonic spirits. A spiritual body, then, would be a body under the influence of the Holy Spirit's activity. It would be a body raised by the Holy Spirit and controlled entirely by him. For that reason F. F. Bruce paraphrased verse 44 to read, 'What is sown is a body animated by the soul; what is raised is a body energized by the Spirit.'[1] When Christ returns, therefore, every Christian will receive a spiritual body, a Spirit-enlivened, Spirit-empowered, and Spirit-led body.[2]

The foundation for this hope lies in Christ, the 'last Adam.' God raised him from the dead and he became 'a life-giving spirit.' When we look at this description and read it in light of Paul's overall argument and emphasis on the spiritual body, it becomes evident that we should capitalize the 'S' as a reference to the Holy Spirit. By God's creative power, Adam was a living being. By God's resurrection power, however, Christ has become the life-giving Spirit.

That description, however, raises a serious question. Has Paul suddenly abandoned an orthodox doctrine of God? Did he collapse the Spirit into the Son and reduce the Trinity to a duality? We should not think that Paul's statement in any way reflects a change in or a confusion about the three distinct persons in the Godhead. It does, however, demonstrate the profound and inseparable link between Christ and the Holy Spirit in the transformative work of salvation and resurrection that characterizes the last days.

---

[1] Bruce, *Letters of Paul*, 117.

[2] Gaffin, *Resurrection and Redemption*, 85-86. Throughout this section I am indebted to the exegesis of Gaffin, Geerhardus Vos, *The Pauline Eschatology* (Phillipsburg, NJ: Presbyterian and Reformed Publishing, 1986), 166-71, and Ridderbos, *Paul: An Outline*, 539-45. Their redemptive-historical understanding of 1 Corinthians 15:35-49 undergirds the above exposition.

Through his resurrection and ascension, Christ poured out the Spirit at Pentecost (see Acts 2:32, 33). The Holy Spirit 'resurrects' souls from spiritual death to new life in Christ (Eph. 2:1-7). New life in Christ is life in the Spirit. So close is the connection between the two persons that Scripture says the Holy Spirit lives in our hearts (Rom. 8:9, 11; 1 Cor. 6:19; 2 Tim. 1:14) and so too does Christ (Rom. 8:10; 2 Cor. 13:5; Gal. 2:20; Eph. 3:17; Col. 1:27) because the Spirit of Christ dwells in us (Rom. 8:9; Gal. 4:6; 1 Pet. 1:11).

The same Holy Spirit who raised Jesus from the dead and 'raised' our souls will one day raise our bodies. Paul combined both of these ideas in Romans 8 where verses 9-11 present us with an exposition of what it means for Christ to be a life-giving Spirit: 'You, however, are not in the flesh but in the Spirit, if in fact the Spirit of God dwells in you. Anyone who does not have the Spirit of Christ does not belong to him. But if Christ is in you, although the body is dead because of sin, the Spirit is life because of righteousness. If the Spirit of him who raised Jesus from the dead dwells in you, he who raised Christ Jesus from the dead will also give life to your mortal bodies through his Spirit who dwells in you' (Rom. 8:9-11).

Believers suffer and die. With natural bodies under the impact of the curse, we are sown in decay, dishonour, and weakness. Because of Christ, however, the Spirit of God brings us to salvation and will one day raise us with imperishable bodies in glory and with power.

Order

Paul describes the transformation that will occur on the day of resurrection and grounds that hope in a robust and thorough-going conception of the covenantal, redemptive-historical movements in Scripture. With that sense of history and eschatology, which were so crucial for his theology, Paul concludes this section in verses 46-49 by focusing on the order of the change.

Because Christ is the last Adam and because the Spirit-raised, Spirit-empowered body so far exceeds our natural bodies, we may be tempted to think the spiritual body came first in God's plan. To draw that conclusion, however, would lead us in the wrong direction and prevent us from seeing the significance of the order as Paul explains it in verses 46-49.

The natural body precedes the spiritual body. 'But it is not the spiritual that is first but the natural, and then the spiritual' (verse 46). Adam came before Christ, and that order is important. Adam was created without sin and, had he obeyed God, the Lord would have confirmed him in righteousness, given him access to the tree of life, and all of his descendants would have enjoyed the blessedness of a godly life forever. That was the order. The natural would have been elevated to the spiritual. As the *Westminster Confession of Faith* describes it, this was the life 'promised to Adam, and in him to his posterity, upon condition of perfect and personal obedience' in the covenant of works.[1] This life was not merely the continuation of a natural and physical existence but life in an immutable and incorruptible glory, the kind of life Revelation 22:1-5 describes.

Adam's sin, however, necessitated the work of Christ. The Lord banned Adam from the tree of life because of his rebellion. It took Jesus and his perfect obedience to the law of God to gain access for us to the tree of life. Where the first Adam failed, the last Adam succeeded. Where the first Adam earned death, the last Adam earned everlasting life. The natural came first and, corrupted by sin, was destined to perish. The spiritual came last, and the spiritual is the Spirit-wrought life of the resurrected Jesus experienced by all those who are in him destined for the new creation.

Once Paul establishes the order, he wants to remind his readers once again of the nature of these bodies he describes. 'The first man was from the earth, a man of dust; the second man is from heaven' (verse 47). God created Adam from the dust of the ground (Gen. 2:7). The Lord designed him for an earthly existence, and dust and earth characterize that existence.

Christ, the second man, is 'from heaven.' If we look at the contrasting descriptions the apostle uses

---

[1] *Westminster Confession of Faith* (7.2), 39.

throughout this section, then it becomes evident that 'from heaven' is not a description of Christ's pre-existence with the Father in glory. As true as that is, it is not Paul's point. He is intent to emphasize that just as dust characterized the first man's existence, a Spirit-empowered and heaven-adapted existence characterizes the Lord Jesus. So much is that the case that Christ in his glorified body ascended into heaven and is now enthroned at the Father's right hand.

Paul, however, never thought of Adam and Christ in isolation from the people they represented. He concludes, therefore, in verses 48, 49 by linking the order and nature of these respective men to their people. Everyone faces the destiny of his or her covenant head. 'As was the man of dust, so also are those who are of the dust, and as is the man of heaven, so also are those who are of heaven. Just as we have borne the image of the man of dust, we shall also bear the image of the man of heaven' (verses 48, 49).

Because Adam is the covenant head of all humanity, those of the dust bear his image (verses 48a, 49a). Their destiny is to perish in dishonour and weakness (verses 42, 43). If Christ, however, is our covenant head, then we will bear his image. God will raise us in his likeness to bear the image of the man of heaven (verses 48b, 49b). In other words, Christ 'will transform our lowly body to be like his glorious body, by the power that enables him even to subject all things to himself' (Phil. 3:21).

In light of this truth, the key question must be, 'Are you in Adam or are you in Christ?' What is your destiny? Is it to perish eternally in your sin and unbelief, or is it to be raised in glory and everlasting life? How can you know if Christ is your Saviour, your covenant head? You can know if you are willing to trust him for your salvation. The Lord Jesus stands as the representative for all those who place their faith in him. If you receive Christ, if you commit the hope of your eternal salvation into his gracious and loving hands, then you can rest assured you will be raised in him and bear the image of the man of heaven.

This assurance isn't just for the hereafter. If Christ is the firstfruits of the resurrection (verses 20, 23) and the age to come has already broken into the present, if we share in life in the Spirit, then our calling is to live in the power of the resurrection. Salvation is about beginning the resurrection life now. In Ephesians 2 Paul wrote, 'But God, being rich in mercy, because of the great love with which he loved us, even when we were dead in our trespasses, made us alive together with Christ—by grace you have been saved—and raised us up with him and seated us with him in the heavenly places in Christ Jesus, so that in the coming ages he might show the immeasurable riches of his grace in kindness toward us in Christ Jesus' (Eph. 2:4-7).

The Lord has saved us to be displays or trophies of his grace. When you see a trophy sitting on a shelf, you know a lot of hard work stands behind it. If the trophy is an award for athletic prowess or musical talent, then you can be sure hours and hours of practice, self-discipline, and focus led to that award. Our new lives in Christ and our coming life in glory will display for all to see the immeasurable riches and the sheer unbounded greatness that stands behind our salvation in the heart of God and the work of the Lord Jesus. The day of Christ is coming when he will be glorified in all his saints (cf. 2 Thess. 1:9, 10).

In light of this resurrection hope, we strive to know Christ and walk in godliness because we are already citizens of the kingdom to come. Paul daily pressed 'on toward the goal for the prize of the upward call of God in Christ Jesus,' and he urged the Philippians to do the same (Phil. 3:14, 15). He wanted them to live for something more because 'our citizenship is in heaven, and from it we await a Saviour, the Lord Jesus Christ, who will transform our lowly body to be like his glorious body, by the power that enables him even to subject all things to himself' (Phil. 3:20, 21).

Don't be shaken by the trials and tribulations you face. Don't be shaken by the unbelief and scepticism that attack the church. Don't be shaken by those who deny the truth. Stand firm because Christ is the life-giving Spirit. We will be raised, this we know, for the Bible tells us so!

6

THE GREAT TRANSFORMATION

1 CORINTHIANS 15:50-58

I tell you this, brothers: flesh and blood cannot inherit the kingdom of God, nor does the perishable inherit the imperishable. [51] Behold! I tell you a mystery. We shall not all sleep, but we shall all be changed, [52] in a moment, in the twinkling of an eye, at the last trumpet. For the trumpet will sound, and the dead will be raised imperishable, and we shall be changed. [53] For this perishable body must put on the imperishable, and this mortal body must put on immortality. [54] When the perishable puts on the imperishable, and the mortal puts on immortality, then shall come to pass the saying that is written:

'Death is swallowed up in victory.'

[55] 'O death, where is your victory?
O death, where is your sting?'

[56] The sting of death is sin, and the power of sin is the law. [57] But thanks be to God, who gives us the victory through our Lord Jesus Christ.

[58] Therefore, my beloved brothers, be steadfast, immovable, always abounding in the work of the Lord, knowing that in the Lord your labor is not in vain.

No doubt you've heard the expression, 'He is so heavenly minded he is no earthly good.' You may even sympathize with those words if you've had to work with someone who always had his head in the clouds and couldn't seem to focus on the project at hand. Don't confuse absent mindedness, however, with heavenly mindedness. The two are by no means the same.

Critics have often used the heavenly-minded and earthly-good contrast to combat a robust doctrinal or theological Christianity. Their attitude sounds something like this: 'People who think and talk about theology are heavenly-minded folks. They like to read, debate, and argue the finer points of doctrine, and that's just a waste of time. What we need are practical Christians! The world needs believers with a faith that does some earthly good, a faith that meets the real needs of real people, a faith that isn't afraid to get its hands dirty.'

Is that, however, the attitude we discover in the New Testament? Do the apostles ever present us with a practical Christianity divorced from a thoroughgoing theological Christianity? The answer is No. Bible students have long observed that Paul's letters follow a fairly common format in which the apostle spends the first half of his correspondence laying out a doctrinal foundation and framework for the church to which he is writing. Only then, in the second half of the letter, does he flesh out the implications of that doctrine for the life of the congregation. Paul and his fellow apostles understood that to be of any earthly good believers first had to be heavenly minded. Christians need a solid theological foundation if they are to serve the Lord and others in practical ways because what we believe affects the way we behave. This lesson is nowhere more evident than in the closing verses of 1 Corinthians 15.

In the last chapter, we followed Paul's argument regarding the resurrection body. It will be an imperishable body, one raised in power and glory like Christ's (verses 42-49). Those affirmations, however, naturally raise the question, 'What about those who are alive when Jesus returns?' Paul's answer is that the day of resurrection is also the day of transformation and victory over death (verses 50-58). The apostle's argument is simple: on the final day, every believer, both living and dead, will be transformed to inherit the kingdom. This future hope of triumph over death has, in turn, the most practical implications for the life of the church. The resurrection day is a day of transformation and victory, and that hope should motivate us, inspire us, and, impel us to fidelity and service. Paul looks at this principle from three angles. He begins with the mystery of our transformation.

The mystery of our transformation

Paul writes, 'I tell you this, brothers: flesh and blood cannot inherit the kingdom of God, nor does the perishable inherit the imperishable' (verse 50). These words are a restatement of the general principle he teaches earlier in verses 42-49. We, like our father Adam, have natural bodies. To live in the heavenly state, however, we need spiritual bodies like Christ's. The natural body, flesh and blood, cannot inherit the kingdom. Though Paul often uses the noun 'flesh' to refer to our fallen nature, that which is 'fleshly' within us (see, e.g. Rom. 7:14; 8:4; Gal. 5:16), here *flesh* is a reference to the physical composition of the human body. That becomes evident because of its association with blood. 'Flesh and blood' describes our present condition as human beings with bodies that die and decay under the curse of sin. This is human existence as we know it.

Writing in a style reminiscent of Hebrew poetry, the apostle restates his point in similar terms: 'nor does the perishable inherit the imperishable' (verse 50b). Flesh and blood are perishable. They are capable of death and decay (cf. Rom. 8:21; 1 Cor. 15:42). They are temporary (cf. Col. 2:22). Our bodies waste away, die, and disintegrate. Because of its association with decay and corruption, the term *perishable* can have definite moral overtones (2 Pet. 1:4; 2:19). The perishable is the corruptible, and one reaps corruption from sowing to the flesh rather than to the Spirit (Gal. 6:8). The kingdom of God, however, is imperishable. The imperishable is incapable of death or decay. God's kingdom will endure forever. Its eternal and incorruptible character requires, therefore, that everyone who enters it must likewise not be subject to death. In other words, an incongruity exists between our current physical condition and the nature of the eternal state in the new creation. This incongruity cannot be compromised, otherwise the kingdom would no longer be the kingdom of God, a kingdom over which he reigns and which bears his eternal and righteous character.

After stating his main thesis in the negative, Paul makes a second assertion to overcome the conundrum he proposes. If, indeed, we cannot inherit the kingdom in our present condition, then how can we ever inherit it since, on our own, we can never cease to be what we were created to be—humans made up of flesh and blood? The apostle's solution is nothing less than a mystery. When you hear the term *mystery*, you may think of the famed detective Sherlock Holmes or a favourite movie. In a mystery story, one attempts to piece together a series of clues to solve a crime. A biblical mystery, however, cannot be unravelled by human ingenuity. Paul didn't pose mysteries to his readers as cases to be cracked but as revealed truths to be accepted.[1] A biblical mystery is knowledge one can possess only by divine revelation.

What is this mystery Paul received from God? It is the knowledge that not every believer will sleep, but everyone will be changed (verse 51). We encountered *sleep* as a metaphor for death earlier in 1 Corinthians 15 (see verses 6, 20). Believers are those who, when they die, fall asleep in Jesus (cf. John 11:11; Acts 7:60; 1 Thess. 4:13-15). Not everyone, however, will die before Christ returns. Many Christians will be alive at the second advent. Those who have died will be raised. They will have spiritual bodies equipped for the kingdom. Those who are alive on that day will be changed. Believers who greet Christ at his second coming will have their bodies transformed from perishable, corruptible flesh and blood to imperishable, incorruptible bodies prepared for eternal life. These Christians will not have to pass through the gateway of death to obtain a glorified, spiritual body like those who will be raised.

Next, in verse 52, Paul describes how and when this change will take place, and he uses three phrases to do so. First, believers living when Jesus returns will have their bodies transformed 'in a moment.' The term translated *moment* is *atomos*. It occurs only here in the

---

[1] The noun 'mystery' occurs primarily in Paul's letters (Rom. 11:25; 16:25; 1 Cor. 2:1, 7; 4:1; 13:2; 14:2; 15:51; Eph. 1:9; 3:3, 4, 9; 5:32; 6:19; Col. 1:26, 27; 2:2; 4:3; 2 Thess. 2:7; 1 Tim. 3:9, 16.). The apostle links mystery closely with revelation (Rom. 16:25; Eph. 3:3; cf. Col. 1:26) and knowledge (1 Cor. 13:2; Col. 2:2).

New Testament and is the origin of the English term *atom*. It is the smallest indivisible particle of time.[1] If Paul were writing this today, he might describe the time it takes for this change to occur as a nanosecond.

Second, the change will happen 'in the twinkling of an eye.' This phrase describes the slightest movement detectable in the human eye or perhaps a blink or glance.[2] The point of these first two expressions is to emphasize how quickly the transformation will occur. Paul does not envision an evolutionary progress which eventually renders the human body capable of inhabiting the new creation. Sanctification, our growth in grace and holiness, is a slow and often painful process. We inch forward day after day as we strive, with the Spirit's power, to become more like the Lord Jesus. Our glorification, however, will be instantaneous.

If the first two phrases combine to describe the suddenness and rapidity of the body's transformation, the third phrase, 'at the last trumpet,' answers the question *When?* The Scriptures associate the sound of a trumpet with Christ's second advent (cf. 1 Thess. 4:16). This concept was not a new idea to the apostle Paul. With his rich background in the Hebrew Bible, he knew that trumpet blasts often

---

[1] William F. Arndt and F. Wilbur Gingrich, *A Greek-English Lexicon of the New Testament and Other Early Christian Literature* (Chicago: University of Chicago Press, 1957), 120.

[2] Morris, *First Corinthians*, 233.

marked celebratory occasions of both rejoicing and victory.[1] See, for example, the feast of trumpets (Lev. 23:23-27; Num. 29:1) and the day of atonement (Lev. 25:9) as well as the victories of Joshua at Jericho (Josh. 6:1-21) and Gideon's defeat of the Midianites (Judg. 7:19-23). Furthermore, the prophets predicted the future triumph of Messiah as the day when the trumpet will be blown (see Isa. 27:13; Zech. 9:14).

In the book of Revelation, the apostle John receives a vision of seven trumpets given to seven angels (see Rev. 8:2, 6, 13). The seventh trumpet is, therefore, the last one to sound. When it is blown, Christ will return for the consummation of the ages and the inauguration of the eternal state. John writes, 'Then the seventh angel blew his trumpet, and there were loud voices in heaven, saying, "The kingdom of the world has become the kingdom of our Lord and of his Christ, and he shall reign forever and ever"' (Rev. 11:15).

The last trumpet announces the last day. When, therefore, the trumpet sounds, then in a split second, faster than you can blink your eye, the dead will rise imperishable. They shall never die again, and the living will experience a metamorphosis. The *Westminster Confession of Faith* describes this transformation with these words: 'At the last day, such as are found alive shall not die, but be changed: and all the dead shall be

[1] *Ibid.* See, e.g., Lev. 25:9; Josh. 6:5, 20; Judg. 3:27; 7:18; Psa. 81:3.

raised up with the self-same bodies, and none other, although with *different qualities*, which shall be united again to their souls for ever.'[1]

The day of Christ's return will be so momentous the human mind cannot adequately grasp all it will involve. Language seems to fail us. We do know, however, that after the Saviour comes again we will not die. Our bodies will not perish nor be subject to corruption, and we will no longer sin. We will be raised in glory and power (see verse 43). We will be different than we are now.

The most wonderful thing about the last day, however, is that we will be like Jesus. Our goal every day should be to follow the Saviour's example (1 Pet. 2:21-25) and bring every thought into captivity to him (2 Cor. 10:5). As we mortify our sin, we want to experience something of the victory that awaits us (Rom. 6:11). But then, on that day, in an instant, we will be completely, entirely, and perfectly like Jesus. When the final trumpet sounds, the dead will not have an advantage over the living nor the living over the dead. Both will receive their Spirit-transformed bodies made fit for the kingdom, and we will be forever with the Lord.

When we compare this passage with others, such as 1 Thessalonians 4:13-18 and Revelation 11:15, it becomes clear the events Paul and John describe usher in eternity. The sound of the trumpet, the resurrection

---

[1] *Westminster Confession of Faith*, (32.2), 164. Emphasis added.

of the dead, the rapture of the saints, the great transformation, and the supreme rulership of Christ over all creation for all eternity occur at the same time.

As a young teenager fascinated by the Bible, I purchased a prophecy chart for my bedroom wall. It was fancy and colourful. It had the future laid out in a series of ages that included intricate details leading up to the second coming of Christ. The longer I have lived with the Bible, however, the simpler my prophecy chart has become. When our Saviour was born, he entered this present evil age. When he died and rose again, he inaugurated the age to come. By his resurrection as the firstfruits (see verses 20, 23), the coming age burst into the present age. In Christ, we now experience the tension of living between the already of Jesus' victory over sin and death and the not yet of the future consummation of the kingdom. The one event that lies between the already and the not yet is his return. My prophecy chart no longer has a series of multiple orderly partitions to describe events prior to the new heavens and new earth. It has one momentous, earth-shattering, transformative event—the second coming of Jesus.

The victory of our transformation

As Paul advances his explanation of the coming great change in verses 53-57, he looks at the day of Christ's return from a second angle and proceeds to explain the mystery of our transformation in terms of victory. Though he repeats the same basic concepts regarding the change to take place in the believer's body and even uses some of the same vocabulary, the transformation the apostle describes culminates in final victory over death itself. If you look closely at these verses, you will see three descriptions of this victory.

First, it is a necessary victory. The necessity of change, of bodily transformation, has been integral to Paul's argument since verse 36. It especially comes to the fore in verses 50-52 since flesh and blood cannot inherit the kingdom. In verse 53, however, Paul is explicit: 'For this perishable body must put on the imperishable, and this mortal body must put on immortality.' It is absolutely necessary for the present perishable body to put on the imperishable and for the mortal body to put on the immortal. The body subject to death and decay must be clothed with a body that cannot fall under the power of death. No alternative exists. The human body, as it is currently constituted, cannot enter the kingdom of God.

Paul not only states the necessity of this change, but he also gives his readers some insight into its nature. It is like putting on a new garment. The phrase *put on* means to be clothed with. One takes off an old robe to be wrapped in a new one. Paul often uses clothing imagery to describe the process of sanctification. For example, believers are to cast off the works of darkness and put on the Lord Jesus Christ (Rom. 13:12, 14). Christians are to put on the new self (Eph. 4:24; Col. 3:10), compassionate hearts (Col. 3:12), and the whole armour of God (Eph. 6:11, 14; cf. 1 Thess. 5:8). In this passage, he utilizes the same pictorial language to describe the believer's glorification. The old garment is flesh and blood, life and death in this world. Our old ensemble will perish and decay. But our new garment is incorruptible and immortal. The old robe is a mantle of death, but the new one is a cloak of everlasting life.

Second, it is a Scripture-fulfilling victory. When the great transformation occurs at Christ's return, 'when the perishable puts on the imperishable, and the mortal puts on immortality,' then God's word will be fulfilled. Paul's reference to 'the saying that is written' (verse 54) points to two prophets of the old covenant: Isaiah and Hosea. Paul first draws an expression from Isaiah 25:8, 'Death is swallowed up in victory' (verse 54). To appreciate his use of the prophet's words, we have to understand the context of what Isaiah wrote. Isaiah 25 occurs in a section of the book often referred to as 'the little apocalypse' (chapters 24–27). Those chapters exalt the Lord as the sovereign in judgment and salvation. God will judge the whole earth, and none will escape (chapter 24), and he will also save his people (chapter 25). In his perfect, unfailing faithfulness, he not only brings destruction (Isa. 25:2) but also deliverance (Isa. 25:3-5). He will provide a feast on Mount Zion (Isa. 25:6), a banquet the New Testament calls 'the marriage supper of the Lamb' (see Rev. 19:6-9). When the Lord hosts that feast, he will swallow up death forever and cause everyone to rejoice. He will wipe away every tear and remove every shame and disgrace (Isa. 25:7, 8). When we survey the context of the passage, it is easy to see why Paul chose it and found so much comfort in it. What is unique about this text is it represents the only occasion in which Paul quotes an unfulfilled prophecy.[1] Most of his appeals to the Hebrew Bible are to demonstrate how Christ's first coming occurred just as the prophets had predicted, but he was certain that the Saviour's second coming would be fulfilled according to the divinely predicted plan as well.

Next, Paul raises two rhetorical questions from Hosea 13:14. Understanding the context of this verse is essential to grasping the reason Paul quotes it. Hosea's marriage to Gomer is a graphic and painful metaphor of Israel's relationship to God. The people of God had been unfaithful to him (Hos. 1:1–3:5) and would be judged for their rebellion (Hos. 4:1–10:15). The Lord loved Israel, however, just as Hosea loved his wife (Hos. 11:1-11), even though they were a sinful and adulterous people (Hos. 11:12–12:14). Hosea 13 continues the sad story of Israel's idolatry and impending judgment, and the Lord calls upon death and the grave to come to his

---

[1] Fee, *First Corinthians*, 803.

aid. Would he spare his wayward people any longer? Would he ransom or redeem them yet again? No, the day of compassion was over. The Almighty summons death to spread its plague and for Sheol to inflict its sting (Hos. 13:14).

Paul uses this passage from Hosea in an interesting way. In the prophet's original context, the questions posed by God are rhetorical and call for death and Sheol to inflict their chastisements. When the Lord asked, 'O Death, where are your plagues? O Sheol, where is your sting?' he called for both death and the grave to come with full force and punish wayward Israel. The apostle, however, turns these questions in a different direction and poses them from this side of the cross. Now that Christ has come, Paul looks back at Hosea and the events surrounding God's judgment through the lens of Calvary. He heard God's summons to death and the grave to punish his people, and he saw their power and pain fall on Jesus. The apostle knows that the Saviour has suffered death and the grave in the place of his people. From that vantage point, rather than calling for death and Sheol to visit with their destructive power, he asks where their victory and sting are? Where will they be found on the day of resurrection and transformation? With a rhetorical flourish, Paul transforms God's summons to death into a gospel-infused taunt! Death and the grave were victorious when the Lord called on them to judge his disobedient people, but when Christ returns to raise, transform, and glorify his saints these great enemies will not win.

Death has a sting. If you have ever been stung by a bee, then you have experienced the sharp, sudden, and intense pain it inflicts. More than a nudge, a push, or a bump, a sting causes penetrating and searing discomfort. Paul sees death's sting as its victory. It triumphs when it inflicted its pain, and the source of its pain is sin (verse 56). Death entered the world through sin (Gen. 2:15-17; 3:19). Sin, and the wrath due to it from a holy and righteous God, makes death a fearful thing (cf. Heb. 2:15). For those whose sin is punished in death, the sting of God's inflicted wrath will last forever.

Where does sin get its power to inflict such pain in death? It derives its power from the law. Though it may at first seem almost blasphemous to say, the law possesses an ability to provoke sin. This power does not arise from an inherent flaw in the law itself. The law is holy, just, and good (see Rom. 7:12). When the stipulations of God's law stand before a sinful heart, however, the iniquitous bent of the human soul says, 'I want what is forbidden.' If you tell a child he can't have a cookie before dinner, then he wants a cookie all the more. When you tell a person not to lie, the human heart wants to deceive. When the law says, 'Do not covet,' our desires kick into full gear and say, 'I want it!'

'But thanks be to God!' When the situation looks its bleakest, Paul finds reason to praise the Lord. If Christ had not been resurrected, everyone would still be lost in sin, hopeless for time and eternity (see verses 11-19). 'But in fact Christ has been raised from the dead' (verse 20). Sin and death are powerful and painful, 'But thanks be to God, who gives us the victory through our Lord Jesus Christ' (verse 57).

The apostle concludes this section with thanks to the Lord because of victory through Christ. Though the law, sin, and death are all arrayed against us, Christ graciously gives us the victory. When faced with the righteous requirements of the law, he obeyed perfectly. When faced with the sting of death because of our sin, he willingly brought himself under its pain and power. Now that the sting has been inflicted on the Saviour, we have the victory over death! Paul draws this same conclusion at the end of Romans 7, 'Wretched man that I am! Who will deliver me from this body of death? Thanks be to God through Jesus Christ our Lord' (Rom. 7:24, 25). For this reason he continues into Romans 8 to declare, 'There is therefore now no condemnation for those who are in Christ Jesus. For the law of the Spirit of life has set you free in Christ Jesus from the law of sin and death' (Rom. 8:1, 2).

How thankful are you for God's gracious, victorious gift of salvation? To be thankful, you have to be intentional to recall, to rehearse, to meditate on the person and work of Jesus. When cultures observe thanksgiving or harvest celebrations, a key element of the festivities involves reflection on the blessings of the past year. How do you develop this kind of reflective attitude? One way is to read and pray through some of the key passages in the Bible about the sufferings of Christ, passages like Psalm 22, Isaiah 53, and the passion narratives in the Gospels. As you meditate, write down what that particular passage has to say about the Lord Jesus and what he has done or endured for you to be saved. Then turn that list into a catalogue of praise.

The challenge of our transformation

Finally, in verse 58, Paul spells out the implications of the coming great change, and these implications present us with the challenge of our transformation. Some may be tempted to think that since the resurrection day awaits us, we should just sit back, take it easy, and wait for Jesus to come again. Because his return is our escape plan, we shouldn't be too worried about trying to maintain or advance the kingdom here and now. Just be ready to meet him! Paul, however, never tolerates such a lackadaisical attitude. Now is not the time to relax but the time to stand firm and move forward. Christ's second coming does not provide believers with an excuse for indolence but with a motive for diligence. 'Therefore, my beloved brothers, be steadfast, immovable, always abounding in the work of the Lord' (verse 58). To be steadfast is to stand firm and not waver but persevere. Paul calls for the Corinthians to be resolute and loyal in their service to God. He also encourages them to be immovable. This adjective occurs only here in the New Testament, and it means to be steady and resolute, or as the NIV translates it, 'Let nothing move you.'

The church constantly faces pressure to compromise its faith and accommodate itself to prevailing trends in the culture. In Corinth, the pressure was to compromise the doctrine of the resurrection. Paul stands firm against this theological deviation because to deny or weaken the doctrine of the believer's future resurrection was to undermine the gospel itself. This is the force of his argument in the first third of chapter 15 (verses 1-19). Christians can agree to disagree among themselves over various points of interpretation, just as some of my friends and I do not see eye-to-eye regarding our prophecy charts. When it comes to the fundamentals of the faith, however, we cannot budge an inch. It is one thing to debate the timing and sequence of events surrounding Christ's second coming, but it is an altogether different issue to deny that Jesus will return. The church must maintain its core beliefs about the nature of God, the inspiration and character of the Bible, the person and work of Christ, and justification by faith alone as expressed in the great ecumenical and Reformation creeds and confessions. Otherwise, the church will end up selling its birthright for a bowl of culturally acceptable stew (cf. Gen. 25:29-34).

Along with the ever-present attacks on the inerrancy of the Bible, the supernatural elements of Christianity, and the gospel itself, the pressure in our day, even from within evangelicalism, is to weaken the church's position on biblical marriage and sexuality. Most of the mainline denominations have capitulated to the culture and have sold out completely with regard to these issues. The Presbyterian Church (USA), for example, openly welcomes practicing homosexuals into membership and ministry.

Evangelical churches have, for the most part, not gone that far—yet. At this juncture, the compromise is more subtle. For example, some people are calling for Christians to embrace their particular sinful tendencies as an essential part of who God made them to be. Hence, some professing believers identify as 'gay Christians.' Sin, however, never defines a man or woman in Christ. If you struggle with heterosexual lust, that does not mean you should embrace 'promiscuous Christian' as your identity. The same is true for any number of other sins. Would you want to be known as a 'thieving Christian,' 'lying Christian,' or 'murderous Christian'? You may well be a believer who struggles with same sex attraction, a desire to steal, deceive, or hate. If so, then you need to repent of your sin and mortify it. You do not need to identify your life with it. This is an area where the church must be steadfast.

Steadfastness does have a downside. If you are resolute in your commitment to Christ and his word, if your congregation remains faithful to the doctrines and practices of historic and biblical Christianity, then you will face accusations of being mean-spirited, harsh, unloving, narrow-minded, and bigoted. In the post, post-modern culture in which we live, many people do not know what to do with a person who has convictions. Because society has become tolerant of every belief, every worldview, and every lifestyle (with the exception of Christianity), for someone to stand up and say, 'Wait a minute, that's wrong!' seems bizarre. The church must identify unbiblical belief systems and ungodly behaviours as sinful, but we must do so with a spirit of compassion for those taken captive by them. We identify sin in order to call sinners to the Saviour. Our calling is to speak the truth in love (Eph. 4:15).

Along with a challenge to gospel fidelity, Paul's concluding inference is also a challenge to diligent labour. The work of the Lord in which we are to abound is the service we offer to our Saviour. God is at work in the world through his church, through the spread of the gospel, and through acts of mercy. The Christian's goal is to enter into the Lord's labours and become co-workers with him and co-workers with our fellow believers (cf.

John 4:31-38). The call to follow the Lord Jesus is always a call to serve, to work for the extension of his kingdom.

What does it mean, however, to abound in this work? To abound is to give yourself 'fully to the work' (NIV). Always strive to excel in your service to Christ. Don't hold back. Don't make excuses. Be willing to take risks (see verses 30-32)! Yes, you should have some idea of your gifts and abilities. Yes, you should know your limitations and not drive yourself to complete exhaustion. But we should work with the utmost devotion.

Those who abound in the Lord's work have the encouragement and assurance that diligent labour for Christ is never wasted effort. You should devote yourself unreservedly to serving the Lord because you know 'that in the Lord your labor is not in vain' (verse 58). With these closing words, Paul circles back to the beginning of the chapter.[1] If members of the church in Corinth reject the resurrection, then they have believed in vain (verse 2), and Paul's preaching has been in vain as well (verse 14). To work by faith in Christ, however, to work with steadfast fidelity to the gospel is never in vain. God will honour, bless, and prosper our work as he sees fit.

Success in the work of the gospel and success for the local church must, however, be judged by the Lord's standards. We tend to think of success in terms

[1] Fee, *First Corinthians*, 808.

of numbers; God thinks of success in terms of faithfulness (see 1 Cor. 4:2). We may work hard for the Lord for many years and still not see done all that we would like, but that does not mean our labour has been in vain.

At the close of the 2019 General Assembly of the Free Church of Scotland, the Moderator, the Rev. Donald G. MacDonald shared the following story. One day the late principal of the Free Church College, the Rev. James Macintosh, summoned MacDonald to his croft, a small highland farm. When he arrived, Mr Macintosh said, 'There's something I want to show you,' and he took him around to the side of the house where a plant was growing. 'That,' he said 'is a hollyhock. There haven't been hollyhocks on this croft in over forty years.' Mr Macintosh then went on to tell how he had a man who helped him on the farm move some soil from further down the croft to the place beside the house where the plant was then growing. He said, 'That seed must have been lying in the soil for over forty years, but given this kind of change of conditions, it's obviously grown.' Then he put his big arm around the Rev. MacDonald and said, 'Most of your life, you will just be sowing the seed of the gospel. You may not see its growth, but your job is just to keep sowing the seed.' Some people plant and some people water, but God gives the increase (see 1 Cor. 3:5-9).

Always abounding in the work of the Lord may not result in fruitfulness measured by crowds or other visible standards of success. Abounding in the work of the Lord means faithfulness. Our calling is to give ourselves fully to God's work wherever that may be and whatever it may involve. The results are up to his sovereign pleasure.

We cannot give ourselves to this kind of work, however, unless we are energized for it by the hope we have in the coming day of resurrection, the day of transformation, the day we see Jesus. May the Lord so keep that hope before us that we will diligently labour on for him. May he be pleased to make us so heavenly minded that we might be of some earthly good!